Clownfishes and other D

Aquarium Success

The complete guide to the successful care and
breeding of these hardy and popular marine fish

Clownfishes and Other Damselfishes

Project Team
Editor: David E. Boruchowitz
Indexer: Elizabeth Walker
Design: Patricia Escabi

T.F.H. Publications
President/CEO: Glen S. Axelrod
Executive Vice President: Mark E. Johnson
Publisher: Christopher T. Reggio
Production Manager: Kathy Bontz

T.F.H. Publications, Inc.
One TFH Plaza
Third and Union Avenues
Neptune City, NJ 07753

Printed and bound in China
10 11 12 13 14 1 3 5 7 9 8 6 4 2

Library of Congress Cataloging-in-Publication Data
Kurtz, Jeffrey.
 Clownfishes and other damselfishes : the complete guide to the successful care and breeding of these hardy and popular marine fish / Jeff Kurtz.
     p. cm.
 Includes index.
 ISBN 978-0-7938-1678-1 (alk. paper)
 1. Anemonefishes. 2. Pomacentridae. I. Title.
 SF458.A45K87 2010
 639.3'772--dc22
                        2010006685

A Note on Measurements: When we convert between American and Metric System measurements, we use rounded-off conversions to provide equivalent levels of precision. Readers familiar with the mathematical concept of significant figures will recognize that these rounded conversions, while less precise, are actually more accurate because they are less precise. Where measurements are only approximate to begin with, as in the nominal gallonage of various standard aquarium sizes (where the actual volume is often quite different from the named size), we use only approximate, round conversions.

The Leader In Responsible Animal Care For Over 50 Years!®
www.tfh.com
CENTRAL
Garden & Pet

Contents

1

Meet the Pomacentrids

Owing to their eye-catching coloration, relatively small size, fascinating (though feisty) behavior, and overall ruggedness, the clownfishes and damselfishes of the family Pomacentridae have long been a mainstay in the marine aquarium hobby. With good reason: these chromatically gifted pomacentrids prove irresistible to novice marine aquarium keepers yet are equally alluring to experienced hobbyists.

Although not normally thought of as a damselfish, the clownfish are members of the same family, Pomacentridae.

All in the Family

This book will introduce you to this diverse family of fishes, offer insights into their natural history, and provide the detailed care requirements you'll need in order to keep them successfully in a home aquarium. If this book is your first glimpse at the clownfishes and damselfishes, allow me to welcome you to a rewarding new fish-keeping experience. And if you're an experienced old salt taking a second look at these fishes, perhaps this book will help to reignite your passion for pomacentrids.

Clownfish or Damselfish: a Distinction Without a Difference?

Though clownfishes are considered damselfishes, a distinction is usually made between these two categories, namely that all clownfishes are damselfishes, but not all damselfishes are clownfishes. The clownfishes are so named for their garish clown-like coloration and comically clumsy swimming movements. Their symbiotic association with sea anemones in nature is well known (though also found in some non-clownfish damsels), and this gives them another common name: anemonefish.

Pomacentrid Taxonomy

The family Pomacentridae consists of four subfamilies, 28 genera, and over 320 species. The subfamily Amphiprioninae, the clownfishes, consists of only two genera, *Amphiprion* and *Premnas*. The subfamily Chrominae contains the genera *Chromis* and *Dascyllus*, and the subfamily Lepidozyginae, the fusiliers, contains only one genus, *Lepidozygus*. The remaining 23 genera are contained within the subfamily Pomacentrinae.

The Shape of Things in Pomacentridae

Members of the family Pomacentridae generally have deep, oval-shaped, laterally compressed (flattened from side to side) bodies; a small terminal (occurring at the end of the head) mouth; an incomplete interrupted lateral line; and a single continuous dorsal fin with 8 to 17 spines and 10 to 18 soft rays. The anal fin typically has two spines, but a few species exhibit three anal fin spines. The caudal (tail) fin of many species is forked to some degree—though not so much among the clownfishes. Most pomacentrids that are of interest to the aquarium hobby stay relatively small, ranging from around 2 inches to around 6 inches (5 to 15 cm) in length at maturity, but there are some much larger species, too.

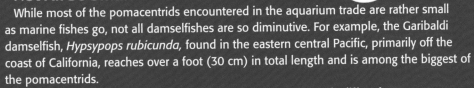

Not All So Small

While most of the pomacentrids encountered in the aquarium trade are rather small as marine fishes go, not all damselfishes are so diminutive. For example, the Garibaldi damselfish, *Hypsypops rubicunda,* found in the eastern central Pacific, primarily off the coast of California, reaches over a foot (30 cm) in total length and is among the biggest of the pomacentrids.

An iconic resident of rocky reefs and kelp forests, *H. rubicunda* differs from most members of its family not only in its rather impressive size but also in the fact that it hails from cool temperate waters rather than tropical coral reefs.

Juveniles of this species have orange-red overall coloration accented by iridescent blue speckles. Mature Garibaldi specimens lose the speckles and are a solid bright orange. Males of the species can be distinguished from females by the presence of a prominent lobe on the head of the male. This impressive pomacentrid was designated the official marine fish of California in 1995.

Although it is common in the trade, few hobbyists can properly keep this species, which requires an aquarium of at least 100 gallons (400 liters) equipped with a chiller.

Don't Get a Complex Over Clownfish Classification

Many non-aquarists and beginning hobbyists alike mistakenly assume that there is only one clownfish species. With its archetypal orange-and-white coloration, *Amphiprion ocellaris* is considered by many to be *the* clownfish. But in actuality there are 28 clownfish species, with 27 belonging to the genus *Amphiprion* and one to the genus *Premnas*. Not all of these species closely resemble the well-known *A. ocellaris*. In fact, there's quite a lot of diversity when it comes to coloration and patterning among the clownfishes.

The various clownfishes are further subdivided into six different groups—called complexes—based on certain physical traits that they have in common. These complexes include (in descending order based on the number of species they contain) the clarkii complex (11 species), skunk complex (six species), tomato complex (five species), saddleback complex (three species), percula complex (two species), and maroon complex (one species).

Don't worry if you're a bit confused by all those clownfish complexes—or by pomacentrid classification in general. Successfully keeping these fishes in a marine aquarium does not depend on having an in-depth understanding of their taxonomy.

Saltwater Cichlids?

Aquarium hobbyists who have a fondness for cichlids might be surprised to discover that the pomacentrids have a lot in common with their favorite freshwater fishes. In fact, both the pomacentrids and the cichlids are grouped in the suborder Labroidei within the order Perciformes. Morphologically, the pomacentrids and cichlids are very similar.

Amphiprion ocellaris is the species most people picture when they think about clownfish, but there are at least 27 other species of clowns.

Also, as anyone who has kept cichlids or damsels can attest, many species from both families take territorial aggression to the extreme, often adopting an entire aquarium for their territory and viciously attacking any intruders—sometimes including fishes much larger than themselves.

Where in the World Do You Find Pomacentrids?

Pomacentrids are found in all tropical seas, usually in association with coral or rocky reefs, with the Indo-Pacific region boasting the greatest abundance of species. A small number of pomacentrid species are found in brackish environments as well. The clownfishes are found in the Red Sea as well as in the Pacific and Indian Oceans.

So Happy Together: Clownfish–Anemone Symbiosis

A clownfish nestled among the tentacles of its host anemone is one of those iconic natural images that many a hobbyist has aspired to recreate in the home aquarium. There's just something undeniably endearing about a tiny clownfish wallowing luxuriously amidst an anemone's potent stinging tentacles without coming to harm, practically daring predators to risk an attack.

In the wild, this symbiotic relationship is an absolute necessity, at least for the clownfishes. With their slow, clumsy swimming movements, they wouldn't stand a chance against the swift-moving predatory fishes strafing the reefs if they didn't have an anemone to retreat to. Exactly how the anemone benefits from the clownfish's presence is not quite as clear, however.

It has been suggested that the host anemone benefits because the clownfish provides nutrition through its waste products as well as any morsels of food that it might drop (whether accidentally or intentionally). However, clownfish-hosting anemones are perfectly capable of sustaining themselves through several mechanisms. Not only are they able to actively sting prey items with the harpoon-like nematocysts (specialized stinging cells) on their tentacles, but they're also able to absorb nutrients directly from the water. Plus, in common with many corals, clownfish-hosting anemones have another nutritional trick up their tentacles—they have photosynthetic algae called zooxanthellae residing in their tissues. These algae utilize energy from the sun to produce nutrients, which they share with their anemone host, thereby allowing the anemone to sustain itself in the very nutrient-poor waters surrounding tropical coral reefs.

The Cichlid Connection

The pomacentrids and the cichlids share a common ancestor, and cichlids are secondarily freshwater fishes, meaning they derive from marine fishes. In fact, several cichlids are found in brackish waters, and a few regularly enter saltwater habitats. Extremely few marine fishes provide parental care of their young—one of the defining characteristics of cichlids; however, one of those few species is a damselfish, *Acanthochromis polyacanthus*, a pair of which herds their fry around just as typical monogamous cichlids do.

Considering all this, it's more likely that the greatest benefit a clownfish provides to its host anemone is not so much its role as breadwinner but, rather, its role as protector. Whereas most fishes are wary of the anemone's sting, some fishes, such as certain butterflyfishes, have a penchant for nibbling on anemones. When a scrappy, territorial clownfish is present, any fish that approaches the anemone looking for a meal will be ruthlessly attacked and driven off by the anemone's resident protector.

What Protects the Protector? But if other fishes regard anemones' stinging tentacles with respect, what makes clownfishes so different? What makes it possible for them to take refuge in a place that would prove painful or deadly to other types of fishes? Extensive research has been conducted on this subject, and numerous theories have been put forth to explain how clownfishes avoid being stung by their anemone hosts.

It has been proposed that clownfishes acquire immunity from an anemone's sting by gradually incorporating some of its mucus into their own mucus coating, thereby rendering themselves chemically indistinguishable from their host. They achieve this by making repeated passes of brief duration through the anemone's tentacles. It has also been suggested that clownfishes alter the chemical composition of their mucus coating when an anemone is present or that they develop an innate protection against an anemone's sting shortly after metamorphosing from larvae to juveniles. However, no one theory seems to hold up entirely when subjected to intensive scientific scrutiny, so it can't be said that there's scientific consensus on the subject. So, for now at least, the exact mechanism—or combination of mechanisms—that gives a clownfish immunity to its anemone host's sting remains a point of contention among experts.

In nature, clownfish need anemones for protection from predators. The benefits of this relationship for the anemone are unclear.

Say "No" to Anemones

The intriguing clownfish-anemone symbiosis is something most beginning aquarists want to replicate in their aquariums. Unfortunately, as hardy and adaptable as clownfishes are, anemones are extremely difficult to keep alive. They are long-lived invertebrates in the wild (with some estimates of ages greater than 200 years) that generally do not live even a few years in captivity. The reasons for this are many, but anemones require extremely exact conditions and are not at all forgiving of an aquarist's shortcomings. Fortunately, clownfish in captivity do just fine without a host anemone. In fact, captive-bred clowns (which is what you should purchase) have never seen an anemone and may not behave normally with one. Resist the temptation to acquire an anemone for your clownfish, at least until you have kept an SPS coral reef system for several years—at which point you may well opt not to try an anemone.

To Each Clownfish Its Preferred Anemone In nature, there are ten sea anemone species that are known to host clownfishes: *Cryptodendrum adhaesivum*, the adhesive sea anemone; *Entacmaea quadricolor*, the bulb-tip anemone; *Heteractis crispa*, the leathery sea anemone; *H. aurora*, the beaded sea anemone; *H. magnifica*, the magnificent sea anemone; *H. malu*, the delicate sea anemone; *Macrodactyla doreensis*, the corkscrew anemone; *Stichodactyla gigantea*, the giant carpet anemone; *S. haddoni*, Haddon's carpet anemone; and *S. mertensii*, Merten's carpet anemone. In some cases *H. aurora* is left off the list, as it hosts only juvenile clownfishes.

Wild clownfishes do not take an any-port-in-a-storm approach to host anemones. In fact, each clownfish species is quite particular about which anemone or anemones it will associate with in the wild. One notable exception is Clark's clownfish, *Amphiprion clarkii*, which is known to associate with all ten clownfish-hosting anemones. The ocellaris clownfish, *Amphiprion ocellaris*, associates with only three anemone species in the wild, *H. magnifica, S. gigantea,* and *S. mertensii.* The maroon clownfish, *Premnas biaculeatus*, is even more finicky, associating only with *E. quadricolor*.

Also, some anemone species seem to appeal to a much greater number of clownfish species than others. *E. quadricolor* and *H. crispa* host 13 and 14 clownfish species respectively, whereas *H. malu* and *C. adhaesivum* each host only one clownfish species— you guessed it, Clark's clownfish.

Among the Coral Branches

Marine aquarium hobbyists and non-hobbyists alike are familiar with the symbiotic relationship that exists between clownfishes and their host sea anemones. But clownfishes aren't the only pomacentrids that associate with reef invertebrates—and sea anemones aren't the only invertebrates that benefit from the presence of a resident pomacentrid. Many damselfish species form close associations with branching stony corals, such as *Acropora* spp. If danger threatens, such as when a predatory fish makes its presence known on the reef, these damsels will dart into the protective branches of their coral head until the threat has passed. While the damsels benefit from the protection provided by the coral's impenetrable cluster of branches, it's believed that the coral benefits from this association, too. The movement of the damsels helps to generate water movement within the coral head, which helps to keep detritus from settling and helps to export the coral's waste products. Furthermore, the waste products of the damsels can serve as a supplemental food source for the corals, which is a boon in the otherwise nutrient-poor waters surrounding coral reefs.

Interestingly, within the confines of an aquarium clownfishes often become less particular about their sea anemone consorts and may adopt a species that they would not normally associate with in the wild. They may also adopt anemone species that don't occur in their natural range, including various *Condylactis* species from the tropical Western Atlantic. As we'll examine in greater detail later in this book, they'll even adopt other non-anemone invertebrates as hosts when no anemone is present in the aquarium.

It's also interesting to note that the clownfishes aren't the only damsels known to take refuge amidst the stinging tentacles of sea anemones. This same behavior is exhibited by at least one non-clownfish damsel species, the three-spot or domino damsel, *Dascyllus trimaculatus*. Well, the juveniles of the species associate with anemones, anyway. This behavior tends to taper off as *D. trimaculatus* matures.

Pomacentrid Social Structure

Social structure takes numerous forms among this large and diverse family of fishes, and, as you'll soon see, the extent to which pomacentrids share (or refuse to share) the areas they occupy on or around the coral reefs has a significant impact on how aggressively they are likely to behave within the confines of an aquarium. Hence it's very important to research the natural social behavior of any pomacentrid before introducing it to your system.

Back to School

Some pomacentrids exhibit schooling behavior—i.e., aggregating in a large group to confuse predators. By banding closely together and choreographing their movements, smaller fishes can decrease the odds that any one individual will fall victim to predation. It's not so easy for a predator to zero in on an individual when it's part of a shifting, shimmering mass, and a synchronized school of fish may appear to be a single larger organism rather than an aggregation of smaller individuals.

The ubiquitous blue-green chromis, *Chromis viridis*, along with various other members of its genus, is an excellent example of a schooling pomacentrid. This species tends to hover above coral heads, snatching zooplankton that drifts by in the water column and dashing into the protective branches of stony corals when danger threatens. *Chromis*, in general, are peaceful pomcentrids, and, unlike so many other marine fish species, they can often be kept successfully in conspecific groups in a

Blue-green chromis are one of the species of pomacentrids that form large schools. This school was photographed off of Heron Island, Australia.

large aquarium provided they are kept in large enough groups, the specimens are all similar in size, and they are all introduced to the tank at the same time.

Staking a Claim

At the other end of the pomacentrid social spectrum you have species that, rather than hang out in relatively peaceful groups, individually stake a territorial claim on a patch of reef and defend it vehemently against competitors for its resources, including members of their own species and any other species that might have designs on the territory's space or food supply. In some cases, individual territories may abut one another to form territorial mosaics.

Individual territory defenders, such as various members of the genus *Stegastes*, the so-called gregories, tend to be either herbivorous or omnivorous in their dietary preference. They also tend to be unholy terrors in captivity, as they commonly adopt an entire aquarium for their territory and may direct their hostility toward all comers, including fishes much larger than themselves as well as the hands of unwary aquarists.

An Invertebrate to Call Their Own

In addition to schooling species and individual territory defenders, there are also pomacentrids that defend a group territory. The clownfishes are, perhaps, the best known among the group territory defenders. A group of clownfish sharing the same host anemone will cooperate to drive away fishes, such as the aforementioned butterflyfishes, that would do their collective host harm. Group territory defense is also observed in certain *Dascyllus* species, such as *D. melanurus* and *D. aruanus*.

These and similar species tend to associate with and shelter in certain branching corals and, like the schooling pomacentrids, feed primarily on zooplankton. Many group territory defenders are long on attitude in the aquarium and must be housed with equally assertive species that can stand up to them. Also, in spite of the fact that they form groups in nature, it's generally not advisable to attempt to keep more than one individual of a group-territory-defending pomacentrid species in the same aquarium. They may get along while still young, but that youthful sociability will often give way to incessant intraspecific squabbling as the specimens mature.

Down on the Algae Farm

Many species of damselfishes exhibit a fascinating environment-modifying behavior that most people wouldn't necessarily associate with fishes. They actually farm plots of algae to feed upon. These damselfishes feed not only directly on the algae in their underwater gardens but also on the various microfauna that are supported by the algae as well as any detritus that gets ensnared in the algae. While they don't plant the algae, they help to create conducive growing conditions for favored varieties by weeding out the forms they don't like to eat. In some cases, damselfishes will also clear a plot where algae can grow by nipping away the living polyps of stony corals. They even assume the role of scarecrow by chasing off any herbivorous fishes or invertebrates, such as tangs and urchins, that attempt to feast on their crop. There is some evidence that a female will select a mate on the basis of how large and luxurious his algae garden is.

Clownfish that share the same anemone will work together to scare off butterflyfish and other threats to it.

Pomacentrids in the Home Aquarium

Their renowned aggressiveness aside, many clownfishes and other damselfishes are ideal candidates for the marine aquarium and are among the best choices for beginning hobbyists. They're readily available on the market and generally quite inexpensive. Most species remain fairly small and demand minimal swimming space. They're not especially fussy eaters, accepting a broad range of standard aquarium fare. Moreover, they are very hardy, holding up remarkably well under less-than-ideal aquarium conditions and shrugging off water-parameter fluctuations that would prove deadly to more sensitive species.

Clowns and damsels are popular fish in the aquarium hobby not only because of their beautiful colors but also because most species are very hardy.

Please, Don't Cycle with Damsels!

Owing to the iron constitution of many damselfishes, they have long been used in the hobby for the utilitarian purpose of cycling a new system—as a source of ammonia to jumpstart colonies of the nitrifying bacteria responsible for biological filtration. While damsels are generally tough enough to withstand moderate levels of ammonia, nitrite, and nitrate, it can't be said that subjecting them to these toxic compounds is a humane practice. Besides, there are better ways to cycle an aquarium that don't depend at all on the use of fishes.

The easiest technique for cycling a new saltwater aquarium is to use the live rock cycling method. As every experienced marine aquarium hobbyist knows—and every hobby newcomer will soon discover—many of the organisms encrusting the live rocks used to aquascape marine systems will die off between the time the rock is collected and the time it is placed into a hobbyist's aquarium. Even rocks that have been pre-cured by the live rock operator will undergo some additional die-off in your aquarium. The ammonia that this die-off produces is more than sufficient to start the cycling process, and quality live rock is sufficiently porous to support abundant colonies of the desired nitrifying bacteria. Therefore all you have to do is monitor the progress of the cycle with quality ammonia, nitrite, and nitrate test kits. Once the ammonia and nitrite levels are zero and the nitrate level begins to spike, the system is considered cycled. Then, after performing a substantial water change to bring the nitrate level down as close to zero as possible, you can safely begin to add livestock.

Apart from the question of whether or not it's humane or ethical to expose a fish to a succession of toxic compounds, there's another reason you don't want to cycle with damsels. As we've already established, many pomacentrids are extremely territorial. So what happens when the first fish introduced to a new system decides to claim the entire tank for its territory, as damsels are likely to do? Well, you can safely assume that any fishes that are subsequently introduced to the tank will get the full brunt of the damsel's aggression—and that's not a good start on the road to a peaceful aquarium community. You're then left with the option of either returning the damsel to your local fish store or temporarily removing it to a quarantine system and attempting to reintroduce it later after the less feisty specimens have had a chance to settle in.

Clownfishes: Practically Perfect for the Home Aquarium

Given their eye-catching coloration, clumsy, waggling swimming movements, endearing behavior, and a boldness that belies their diminutive size, it's not surprising that clownfishes win their way into so many hobbyists' hearts and tanks. In fact, it's the rare beginner who does not include a clownfish in his or her original stocking scheme. And, whereas some of the more stunning marine fish species prove heartbreakingly difficult to maintain in captivity, most of the commonly available clownfishes seem to be ideally suited to life in the marine aquarium.

In nature, clownfish rarely leave the protective tentacles of their home anemone, enabling them to adapt easily to life in a small aquarium.

Most Are Easy Feeders

One of the biggest frustrations marine aquarium hobbyists face is introducing a fish that simply refuses to eat or that eats well at first but then, for some inexplicable reason, decides to go on a hunger strike. In some cases this annoying behavior can persist until the specimen actually perishes from starvation. On the other hand, most clownfishes and most of the other commonly sold pomacentrids seldom refuse to eat what's offered to them. Dry, fresh, and frozen rations are usually accepted with gusto, making it very easy to provide clownfishes with a varied, nutritionally complete diet.

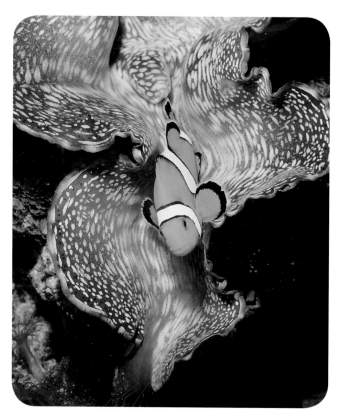

With no anemone for shelter, aquarium clownfish sometimes use a clam or other invertebrate as a host.

Clumsy Homebodies

Keeping certain fast-moving marine fishes, such as the various surgeonfishes, in a small- to medium-sized aquarium is like keeping a racehorse confined to a small pen. It's just not healthy for the fishes to attempt to contain all that energy in such a limited space. Hence most surgeonfishes (a.k.a. tangs) must be kept in larger systems of 75 to 100 gallons (280 to 400 liters) or more and must be provided ample swimming space within the system. In contrast, clownfishes, which in nature seldom swim far from the protective tentacles of their host anemone (and, being slow, clumsy swimmers, would be highly vulnerable to predation if they did), usually do quite well in smaller systems of 20 to 30 gallons (75 to 115 liters).

They're Still Damsels

But don't be deceived by their cuteness. Clownfishes are still damsels, and they've got the attitude to prove it. The percula clownfish, *Amphiprion percula*, that I've had in my 75-gallon (280-liter) reef system for almost 12 years as of this writing never seems to grow weary of attacking my hand whenever I reach into the tank. No matter how vigorously I swipe at it to keep it at bay while I attempt to work in the tank, it always renews the attack—and it seems to know instinctively that it can inflict the greatest amount of pain by nipping at the soft tissue in between my fingers. It's lucky for me that this fish is only a few inches in length and doesn't have formidable teeth. Otherwise, I'd be missing several digits.

Also, be aware that some clownfish species grow quite large (as pomacentrids go, anyway) and will shift their bullying behavior into overdrive as they mature. For example, that wee, adorable tomato clownfish, *Amphiprion frenatus*, which was only about 2 inches (5 cm) when you bought it, will eventually mature into a cantankerous bruiser—exceeding 5 inches (13 cm) in length—and attempt to claim dominion over any fish small or passive enough to be bullied.

No Anemone Required

I've already mentioned the frustrating paradox of clownfish keeping: while most clownfishes adapt remarkably well to living in captivity, the same cannot be said for their host anemones. Very few hobbyists succeed in keeping

A Sampling of Anemone Surrogates

There is no definitive list of invertebrates that clownfishes will try to adopt as a host in the absence of an anemone. But, to a certain extent, the more obviously anemone-like an invertebrate is, the more likely it is that a clownfish will try to settle in it. Corals that have long or fleshy tentacles or stalked polyps generally top the list of likely candidates. Examples of stony corals that might be adopted as surrogates include the very anemone-like plate corals, elegance corals, the various anchor, torch, and frogspawn corals, bubble, or grape, corals, open brain corals, and flowerpot corals, *Goniopora* spp.

Clownfishes may try to settle in certain soft corals, as well. Examples of possible surrogates from this group might include certain leather corals, green star polyps, colt corals, pulse corals, and various mushroom polyps (corallimorpharians). They've even been know to settle into a patch of hair algae or other form of algae when no suitable invertebrate host is available.

An Exception to the Rule

While keeping clownfish-hosting sea anemones in captivity is generally something to be discouraged, there is one possible exception to this no-anemones rule for reef hobbyists who are determined to observe clownfish/anemone symbiosis in their aquariums—the bulb-tip, or bubble-tip, anemone, *Entacmaea quadricolor*. Of all 10 host anemones, this species is the hardiest and adapts to captive conditions most readily. In fact, if given appropriate conditions and care, *E. quadricolor* will readily reproduce via asexual fission in aquariums.

That's not to suggest that keeping *E. quadricolor* is for the average hobbyist, however, and it should definitely not be attempted by beginners. In common with all clownfish-hosting anemones, *E. quadricolor* is photosynthetic and therefore must be provided high-intensity reef lighting if it is to survive. It also demands exceptional water quality, excellent water circulation, and stable water parameters that are as close to natural seawater values as possible. If you are an experienced reefkeeper, you could try to keep this animal with your clowns.

Another key to success with *E. quadricolor* is to offer regular feedings (twice weekly, more or less, depending on the size of the offering) of meaty marine foods.

In addition to reef-quality water and lighting conditions, a system housing *E. quadricolor* should provide ample rockwork so that the specimen can select a suitable crevice to wedge itself in as it would in nature. While roaming about the tank, they can blunder into—and get fatally injured upon—hazards such as powerhead intakes. Steps must be taken to eliminate access to any such dangers. Moreover, if other sessile invertebrates are present in the system, a wandering anemone can come into direct contact with them, potentially resulting in one or the other being stung. Hence, a system housing *E. quadricolor* and other sessile invertebrates must be sufficiently large to allow ample spacing between specimens.

anemones alive in an aquarium for long. In fact, most of these animals, which can live for centuries in the wild, perish within a matter of months in captivity.

Not only does the collection of host anemones virtually ensure that they will have a significantly abridged lifespan, but it also ensures that fewer wild clownfishes will have a place to call home in their natural range. Remember, clownfishes in the wild cannot survive without a host anemone.

So if clownfishes in the wild cannot survive without a host anemone and host anemones seldom survive in captivity, doesn't it stand to reason that clownfishes as well are ultimately doomed in captivity? That's where the good news comes in. Most clownfishes have no need for a host anemone in the aquarium. As a matter of fact, they get along just fine without them. The only reason they depend on them in the wild is to discourage predation, but since the selection of tankmates is entirely within the hobbyist's control, there should be no threat of a clownfish's becoming a meal for a predator within the confines of an aquarium.

Substitute Hosts

Though clownfishes will do just fine in an aquarium absent a host anemone, their instinct to seek a protective invertebrate host must be quite strong, because in reef systems they will commonly adopt surrogate hosts, including various soft corals, large-polyp stony corals, corallimorpharians (so-called mushroom polyps), and other non-anemone invertebrates.

The finger-nipping percula clownfish I mentioned earlier in this chapter actually adopted a giant clam, *Tridacna maxima*, as a surrogate host for a period of several months. The clownfish would settle into the clam's fleshy mantle and chase away any fish tankmates that ventured too close to its adopted host.

While it's fascinating to observe this displaced symbiotic behavior, it's important to be aware that it can create a problem for the surrogate host, which, after all, does not naturally harbor clownfishes. If the adopted invertebrate perceives the clownfish as an irritant, it will respond by closing up whenever the clownfish attempts to take refuge. When this happens continually to a photosynthetic invertebrate it may not receive sufficient lighting to sustain its zooxanthellae and may begin to starve and waste away as a result. If you observe that an invertebrate is refusing to open and you know or suspect that a clownfish has adopted it as a surrogate host, it may be necessary to remove the clownfish from the system.

Tankmate Trouble

Because clownfishes and other damselfishes are so rugged and adaptable to aquarium conditions, the biggest challenges they present to hobbyists are generally related to compatibility. When creating a stocking scheme that includes pomacentrids, it's critical to choose tankmates that will neither harass nor be harassed by the resident clownfish or damselfish.

Pleased to Eat You!

In spite of their feistiness, most pomacentrids remain fairly small, which puts them pretty low on the fish food chain. They may not go down a predator's gullet without a fight, but if they share tank space with a predatory species that has a sufficiently large mouth, they'll eventually end up there nonetheless. That means large predators such as groupers, lionfishes, triggerfishes, and moray eels would definitely not be good choices for tankmates.

And the overall length of a predator isn't the only factor to consider. Some smaller predators as well should be considered off limits as pomacentrid tankmates. For instance, smaller frogfishes that reach only about 4 inches (10 cm) in length might not appear capable of gobbling up a larger clownfish or damsel, but don't be deceived. These cryptic fishes, with their capacious mouths and ravenous appetites, can engulf surprisingly large prey items—including fishes almost as big as themselves!

Minnow-Sized Body, Shark-Sized Aggression

On the other hand, some pomacentrids can be so belligerent for their size that they can turn an otherwise peaceful aquarium community into a war zone, ruthlessly picking at individuals of smaller, more passive species. Some even seem to be of the mindset that the bigger they are, the harder they fall or whatever doesn't eat me makes me stronger, because they'll think nothing of going ballistic on tankmates that are considerably larger than themselves. Needless to say, it's of the utmost importance to research the temperament of any pomacentrid species you plan to keep before you purchase it and then choose its tankmates accordingly, factoring in their natural dispositions as well.

Many *Chromis* species form relatively peaceful schools, and unlike other pomacentrids, do best when kept in groups in the aquarium.

Crab Attack!

Possible compatibility problems aren't limited to the other fish sharing a pomacentrid's aquarium. I once added four emerald crabs, *Mithrax sculptus* (photo below), to a reef system to help bring a bubble algae outbreak under control. The crabs quickly vanished into the rockwork, emerging only after lights out to feed. I didn't give them much more thought (except to observe that they apparently weren't doing much to eradicate the irksome green bubbles—in fact, the problem was actually getting worse on their watch!) until one morning I noticed a rather serious injury on the ocellaris clownfish that resided in the tank. Its anal fin looked as if it had been sheared off, and a big notch had been cut out of its caudal fin.

In no time, the injured fins began to show signs of a secondary infection, which quickly spread to the fish's body. The poor thing looked ghastly—as if the ventral half of its body had been dipped in boiling water. I didn't hold out much hope for its survival. Nonetheless, I transferred the specimen to a hospital tank and treated it with antibiotics. Though its anal fin never grew back, its tail was somewhat misshapen, and the pigmentation in the affected area never quite returned to normal, the clownfish otherwise made a full recovery and lived for several more years.

As for the culprit—or culprits—that had inflicted the injury, I had to systematically capture and remove the emerald crabs, waiting until they emerged to feed after dark, dazzling each specimen with a flashlight, and then quickly snatching them out of the tank with aquarium tongs. It took me several nights to complete my seek-and-capture mission, but once all the crabs had been removed there were no further attacks on the clownfish or any other specimens in the tank.

Careful With Conspecifics

One of the frustrating aspects of marine fish-keeping is that it's seldom possible to keep more than one individual of a given species in the same aquarium, especially if the aquarium happens to be small to medium in size. Even species that form huge schools in the wild often won't tolerate the presence of conspecifics in the aquarium. With a few noteworthy exceptions, the pomacentrids fall under this one-specimen-to-a-tank rule.

Exception: Mated Pair One of these noteworthy exceptions is if you can get your hands on a mated male-female pair. "Mated pair" does not mean any random combining of a male and female, however. Rather, it means two already-bonded mates that were collected together in the wild, kept together through shipping, and sold together as a confirmed mated pair at your local fish store. There are other ways to end up with a mated pair, but we'll explore those techniques more thoroughly in Chapter 8.

Exception: Peaceful Schoolers Another exception is the case of certain relatively peaceful schooling species, such as the various *Chromis* species. Note I did not say "schooling species," but "peaceful schooling species." Many damsels form huge groups in the wild but cannot be kept in groups of any size in the aquarium.

Not only is it possible to keep more than one *Chromis* specimen together, but they actually tend to fare better when kept in groups in the aquarium. However, aggression can be an issue even within such a group. A pecking order develops in the school, with the least dominant individuals receiving the lion's share of the aggression. On the coral reefs, *Chromis* schools are generally large enough that this dominant behavior is diffused among many individuals so that no one specimen takes the full brunt of it. But within the confines of an aquarium, it's not uncommon for smaller, more passive individuals to be pestered to death by more domineering conspecifics—especially when a small group is kept. Hence it's recommended to keep *Chromis* species in groups of at least six, preferably more, and to choose specimens for the group that are all very similar in size.

Not All Damsels Are Devils

With all this talk about the belligerence of clownfishes and other damselfishes, one might be inclined to ask why anyone would want to keep pomacentrids at all if they're so pugnacious. Well, even though many pomacentrids lean toward mean in their disposition, there are some members of the family that are a little more easygoing toward tankmates, such as the aforementioned *Chromis* species. You can also find some relatively peaceful species among the so-called demoiselles of the genera *Chrysiptera* and *Neopomacentrus*.

If you're looking for a peaceful damsel, you really can't go wrong with the yellowtail blue damsel, *Chrysiptera parasema*. This little blue-and-yellow jewel is about as non-aggressive as pomacentrids get and, like the *Chromis* species, can even be kept successfully in groups in bigger systems. The azure demoiselle, *Chrysiptera hemicyanea,* is another peaceful, beautiful member of this genus, which exhibits colors from the

Two of the more peaceful damsel species are *Chrysiptera hemicyanea* (left) and *C. talboti* (right).

same palette as *C. parasema*. Springer's demoiselle, *C. springeri*, with its solid-blue coloration, and Talbot's demoiselle, *C. talboti*, with its bright yellow tones, are also excellent choices.

Among the *Neopomacentrus* species, the regal demoiselle, *N. cyanomos*, the yellowtail demoiselle, *N. azysron*, and the coral demoiselle, *N. nemurus*, are all good choices if you're looking for peaceful damsels, and all can be kept successfully in groups.

Among the clownfishes, the widely recognizable ocellaris clownfish, *Amphiprion ocellaris*, stands out for its relatively peaceful disposition toward non-clownfish tankmates, which is great news for hobbyists since it is also one of the most—if not the most—readily available species in the trade.

Order of Introduction Matters

Even with more peaceful pomacentrid species, the order in which they are introduced to an aquarium community can have an enormous impact on the level of aggression they exhibit toward tankmates. As a general rule, an aquarium should be stocked beginning with the most passive species and ending with the most aggressive. This stocking approach serves two important purposes. One, it gives the less feisty fishes a chance to settle in to their new surroundings and establish a territory without being constantly harassed by more aggressive species. Two, it prevents the more aggressive fishes from claiming the entire tank for their territory and, hence, directing their hostility toward any fish introduced after them. With few exceptions, it's safe to assume that any aggressive pomacentrid should be the last fish introduced to an aquarium community.

Starting With a Clean Slate

So what happens if you've introduced a clownfish or damselfish to your tank, followed it with the introduction of a more passive species, and now the pomacentrid is behaving aggressively toward the newcomer? Does that mean that either the aggressive pomacentrid or the newcomer has to go? Not necessarily—well, not permanently, anyway. When an inappropriate order of livestock introduction results in territorial aggression, there is an intermediate step you can take that is often effective at restoring peace to an aquarium community.

You can try to erase the established territorial boundaries in the aquarium by completely rearranging the rockwork and/or decorations. Doing this is, in essence, like introducing all of the fishes to a completely new system simultaneously so that no individual has the upper hand (fin). Hence all of the specimens, including the aggressive damsel or clownfish, must direct their energies into finding a new territory rather than driving interlopers out of an established one.

If simply rearranging the rockwork isn't effective at mitigating the aggression, don't panic. You're not out of options yet. In this case, you can try removing the pomacentrid from the system for a few weeks by placing it into a separate quarantine tank and then reintroducing it to your display tank after the more passive fish has had a chance to get settled in and establish a territory of its own. If you rearrange the rockwork in the display tank during the pomacentrid's absence, all the better.

This technique isn't effective in all circumstances; if you're dealing with an especially aggressive pomacentrid, it sometimes just succeeds in temporarily postponing the inevitable. Nonetheless, it's worth a try.

The ocellaris clownfish is one of the most readily available species and perhaps the one that is least aggressive to tankmates.

Good Pomacentrid Companions

We've already covered some of the compatibility issues that can arise in aquariums housing pomacentrids, so how can you be sure you're choosing compatible tankmates? As mentioned earlier, larger predators are out of the question and members of the same species, with the few exceptions already noted, should be excluded. So what characteristics should you look for when choosing appropriate companions for a pomacentrid? Make sure the tankmates are dissimilar in appearance and that they match the pomacentrid's level of aggression.

Different Is Good The more similar a species is in shape, size, and color, the more likely it is that a clownfish or damselfish will perceive it as competition for resources—and the more likely it is to be targeted for aggression. Obviously, conspecifics and congeners (members of the same genus) of the pomacentrid are going to be the most similar in appearance and, hence, the most likely to elicit hostility from an aggressive pomacentrid. But you also have to be careful about combining completely unrelated species that happen to share similar color or physical traits. For example, combining the golden damsel, *Amblyglyphidodon aureus,* with the very similarly sized and colored lemonpeel angelfish, *Centropyge flavissima,* might be asking for trouble, especially if the angelfish is introduced after the damsel.

Aggression Match Tankmates for pomacentrids should be very similar in their level of aggressiveness. That is, feisty clownfishes and damselfishes should be housed with species that are equally assertive, and their more passive kin should be housed with species of similar disposition. Remember, this is not just a question of relative sizes. Larger, more passive species can be bullied by much smaller pomacentrids, and passive pomacentrids can be bullied by fishes that are smaller but more aggressive.

Keep It Down Down There!

We tend to think of the undersea world as a silent realm, but some reef fishes can be downright noisy, communicating with their own and other species through a variety of sounds—some actually audible to the human ear. Included among these underwater noisemakers are many of the pomacentrids, which are known to produce various clicking, popping, and chirping noises. Experts believe pomacentrids make these sounds for a variety of reasons, such as attracting a mate, signaling submission during courtship, and frightening off intruders or rivals.

How do pomacentrids produce these sounds? After all, clownfishes and damselfishes don't have a voice box, do they? Actually, they make these percussive pops and chirps by striking their teeth together.

3

Choosing and Housing Pomacentrids

Pomacentrids purchased in good health are about as bulletproof as aquarium fishes can get. But the operative phrase here is "purchased in good health." Unfortunately, these fishes may endure a lot of stress from the time they're captured in the wild until they appear for sale at your local fish store. As a result, when many specimens reach your dealer's shop they may be on the verge of succumbing to disease, injury, ammonia poisoning, or other stressors associated with collection and shipping.

When selecting pomacentrids for your tank, pass over any that are lethargic, hiding, or uninterested in food.

Signs of a Healthy, Happy Pomacentrid

A healthy pomacentrid will have a full, robust body with completely intact fins, vibrant coloration, and clear, non-bulging eyes. It should be swimming actively (though clumsily in the case of clownfishes) and behaving boldly. Most importantly, make sure the specimen is eating as it should. It is seldom difficult to elicit a feeding response from a healthy pomacentrid, so be sure to ask your dealer to feed the specimen right in front of you. If it doesn't eat, pass it by. Period.

Avoid specimens that are listless and lethargic; cowering in the corner of the tank; twitching, trembling, or dashing about nervously; swimming erratically; breathing rapidly; or scraping their bodies against rocks, decorations, or other objects in the tank. Also avoid any specimen that exhibits faded coloration; any obvious injuries, pits, or lesions; ragged, torn, or rotting fins; excessive body slime; a velvety coating or tiny white spots; cloudy or bulging eyes; or a pinched-in belly. Essentially, if any physical or behavioral symptom gives you cause for concern, you're better off bypassing the fish that exhibits them.

And don't limit your health evaluation strictly to the specimen you want to buy. It's important to pay attention to the condition of the other fishes that are sharing its tank, too. If you see other specimens in the same tank that are sick, dying, or dead, it's a pretty safe bet that it won't be long before the specimen you've got your eye on gets sick as well—even if it appears to be perfectly healthy at the moment.

Patience Is a Virtue When Purchasing Pomacentrids

Pomacentrids that spend a few days in a dealer's tank getting acclimated to aquarium conditions and getting accustomed to eating standard aquarium fare before they are purchased tend to have a much better overall survival rate. So do yourself a favor and resist the urge to buy that damsel or clownfish on the same day it arrives. If you're concerned that another customer will buy the specimen you want in the meantime, ask the dealer whether you can put down a little earnest money to hold the specimen for a few days so you can be sure it's healthy.

Resist Those Tiny Discount Damsels!

It's quite common for aquarium stores to offer very small damselfishes for sale at just a few dollars apiece. While these prices may seem like an excellent deal, those tiny discount damsels are really not such a hot bargain, after all—a truth that I had to learn the hard way.

Some years ago I was stocking a new marine aquarium and decided that a school of six blue-green chromis, *Chromis viridis,* would be a great way to introduce some activity and color to the tank. Imagine my delight when I discovered that a dealer in my area was offering blue-green chromis for the low, low price of just $1.99 each. They had just arrived that day, and I was first in line to buy them! How could I resist? Sure, they were only about a half inch (1 cm) in length, but they would grow, right? Besides, the larger specimens in an adjacent tank cost twice as much!

I took my six specimens home and acclimated them very gradually to my quarantine tank, still smug about my substantial dollar savings. The folly of my purchase started to become apparent the next morning when I found one of them dead. No problem, I thought to myself. I've got five chromis left—still enough for a small school. The next day, however, I was down to four. The day after that, only two remained. And then, the following morning, there were none.

The lesson I learned from that disappointing loss, one that has been confirmed many times

A. ocellaris are tank-raised in large numbers for the aquarium hobby. This one has an abnormal pattern.

by the experiences of other hobbyists, is that undersized damsels, however desirably priced they may be, have an absolutely abysmal survival rate because they are simply not resilient enough to endure the rigors of capture, shipping, and handling.

Buy Captive-Bred Clownfishes

On the freshwater side of the aquarium hobby, the vast majority of specimens sold on the market are bred commercially. But just the opposite is true on the marine side of the hobby. The number of species that are still wild caught far exceeds the number of those that are captive bred on a commercial scale.

There's a good reason that so few marine fishes are being bred in captivity. The eggs and tiny larvae of most reef fishes go through a prolonged pelagic stage, during which they drift over many miles of sea with the planktonic rafts. Eventually they reach a stage of development at which they are ready to settle on a coral reef.

This reproductive strategy has the obvious advantage of distributing a species over a very wide range. But, as you might imagine, it also creates lots of headaches for aspiring breeders because little is known about how to sustain such minuscule larvae during this long pelagic stage. Even culturing a food small enough to fit into the tiny mouths of these larvae is problematic. On the other hand, many of the clownfishes are now being commercially bred on a routine basis.

Captive breeding of clownfishes is easier than it is for many other reef fishes because the clownfishes are demersal spawners (they lay their eggs on a substrate rather than in the water column), the larvae are fairly advanced developmentally when they hatch, and the larvae don't have as prolonged a pelagic stage as many other reef fishes do. Because clownfish larvae are relatively large, they are able to accept easily cultured live foods, such as marine rotifers and, later, brine shrimp.

Whenever possible, hobbyists interested in purchasing a clownfish should choose captive-bred specimens over wild-caught specimens. This offers numerous benefits to the hobbyist. They include:

- Captive-bred clownfishes have not had to endure the rigors of capture and prolonged shipping, so they are in much better condition overall when they arrive at your local aquarium store.
- Captive-bred specimens are used to life in captivity—the only life they've ever known! There is no difficulty getting these fish to accept standard aquarium foods.
- Captive-bred clownfishes are less likely than wild-caught individuals to carry diseases or parasites.
- You can also be confident that you're starting with a young specimen. There is no way of knowing whether a wild-caught specimen is just starting out in life or approaching the end of its natural lifespan.

Sometimes captive-bred clownfishes cost slightly more than wild-caught specimens, but they are well worth the price! Wouldn't

The Perfect Introduction to Saltwater Aquariums

Not only are many pomacentrids great fish for novice marine aquarium hobbyists, but they're also a good choice for introducing kids to the responsibilities of marine fish keeping. A smaller aquarium containing a damselfish or, perhaps, a clownfish pair can be set up and maintained with a little parental oversight. After some basic instruction, kids should be able to manage everyday chores, such as feeding, checking the water temperature, and topping off the tank with dechlorinated tap water to compensate for evaporation. Initially, the parents might want to help with some of the more complicated tasks, such as testing for ammonia, nitrite, and nitrate and performing water changes, but even these chores can eventually be learned and mastered by children once they've had an opportunity to observe how they are accomplished. Such a family aquarium is a great educational tool that will help strengthen a child's sense of responsibility—not to mention it may just awaken a lifelong passion for the marine aquarium hobby!

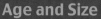

Age and Size

In clownfishes, sex is determined by rank and size is determined by sex. An adult fish will be one of three different sizes. In the wild a small group of juvenile, sexually undifferentiated clowns will occupy an anemone. The dominant fish will become a female and grow to maximal size. The second-ranking fish will become a functional male and grow to the second size. All the rest remain quite small, the third size. If the female is lost, the male will become a female and grow to full size, and one of the small fish will become a male and grow to medium size. It is quite possible for one of the sexually undifferentiated never to become a male or female and to live out its life at the smallest size.

Thus a small clownfish that is wild caught could be a juvenile just establishing itself on the reef, or it could be a geriatric specimen nearing the end of its life.

you rather pay a bit more for a specimen that is far and away more likely to survive in your tank and that wasn't taken from the wild? Consider it an investment in success.

Deadly Harvest: A Note About Cyanide Collection

One very regrettable aspect of the marine aquarium trade is the ongoing use of cyanide poison to stun and capture reef fishes in some areas, such as the Philippines and Indonesia—and, yes, damselfishes (though, to my knowledge, not clownfishes) are among the fishes known to be collected in this manner from these areas.

Cyanide is used for the very simple reason that it facilitates the easy capture of large numbers of fishes with very minimal effort. The fish collector simply squirts the cyanide mixture into the coral heads and crevices where the fishes take refuge and then gathers them up after they become immobilized and sink to the bottom. Because cyanide collection is so much easier than net collection, fishes taken in this manner can be brought to market at a price that is much more attractive to hobbyists.

The problem is that virtually all cyanide-exposed fish perish—many right there on the spot and many more during transportation and distribution. Those that linger long enough to make it into a hobbyist's tank die days or weeks later, leaving the hobbyist guessing what he or she could possibly have done wrong to cause the fish's fatality.

What's worse, cyanide collection doesn't kill only fishes. It also wipes out any invertebrates that are exposed to the poison, which can lead to the loss of entire tracts of coral reef.

Unfortunately, there's no way for the average hobbyist to know just by looking at the fishes in a dealer's display tanks whether or not they were collected by net or via an unsustainable method such as cyanide poisoning. But there are steps conscientious hobbyists can take to ensure that they aren't supporting this ecologically devastating practice. They include:

- Get to know the dealers in your area, and ask them about the source of their livestock. Better dealers should be able to tell you where their fishes come from (remember, fishes collected from the Philippines or Indonesia should be considered suspect) and whether or not they were collected in a sustainable manner.
- As mentioned earlier, purchase captive-bred fishes whenever possible. There's obviously no risk that those specimens have been exposed to cyanide.
- Be willing to pay a few extra dollars for net-collected fishes. An inexpensive fish is no bargain if it dies shortly after purchase.
- If it is available in your area, purchase livestock that has been certified by the Marine Aquarium Council (MAC). MAC certification is your insurance that a fish has been collected, handled, and shipped in a sustainable fashion.

Some collectors use cyanide to catch damsels and other fish, a practice that threatens the survival of coral reefs. Avoid purchasing cyanide-collected fish.

Choosing a Tank for Pomacentrids Is No Big Deal

Having limited space in your home to accommodate an aquarium is not necessarily a limitation on keeping clownfishes and damselfishes. Many are well suited to life in a modest-sized home aquarium in the range of 20 to 40 gallons. Even tanks that would be considered grossly undersized for many other reef fishes can be suitable housing for certain pomacentrid species.

Nice for Some Nanos...

With the burgeoning popularity of nano aquariums—defined for our purposes as systems of 30 gallons or smaller—the demand has risen for marine fishes that can adapt to life in such confined quarters. Many pomacentrids, especially certain smaller clownfish species such as the ocellaris and percula clowns, can be considered reasonable candidates for these smaller systems.

...But Not for All

Not all nano aquariums can realistically support a clownfish or damselfish for

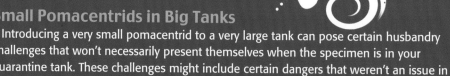

Small Pomacentrids in Big Tanks

Introducing a very small pomacentrid to a very large tank can pose certain husbandry challenges that won't necessarily present themselves when the specimen is in your quarantine tank. These challenges might include certain dangers that weren't an issue in quarantine and that are never experienced in nature. For example, a diminutive damsel can easily be swept into the overflow chamber of a wet/dry biofilter or get stuck on the intake of a powerhead. Any such hazards must be blocked or screened off to prevent accidents.

The high level of water movement that is necessary in a large system can also create problems for a small pomacentrid. Constantly struggling against a very powerful current can exhaust a little damsel or clownfish—potentially stressing it to the point of death. Also, feeding small pomacentrids is more of a challenge in a larger system because the brisk water movement can quickly disperse small food items before the damsel or clownfish sees it. To mitigate these potential problems, it's helpful to provide an area of slack current in the aquarium where the clownfish or damsel can rest and take refuge. To prevent tiny food items from dispersing too quickly, it's a good idea to temporarily unplug your powerheads and pumps at feeding times.

Some of the smaller clownfish, such as ocellaris and percula clowns, will do well in a nano aquarium.

the long term. Don't assume that just because one of these fishes can fit in a very small nano system that it will be healthy and happy there over the course of its life. Pomacentrids can live for well over a decade in captivity, and they deserve the best care we can provide over the course of that long lifespan. So we have to be realistic about the volume of water we attempt to keep them in.

Would a 20- to 30-gallon system suffice for a small to medium-sized pomacentrid, provided it is well maintained and appropriately stocked? Almost certainly. When you move into the 10- to 12-gallon nano range, you're definitely entering borderline territory; although it could be done with meticulous maintenance and attention to water parameters. But a 5-gallon or smaller system? Consider these out of the question for even the smallest clownfish or damsel.

Nano Negatives

Because so many pomacentrids are good candidates for smaller aquariums, it behooves us to examine some of the drawbacks inherent in these systems. These challenges shouldn't necessarily be viewed as deal breakers for the aspiring clownfish or damselfish keeper, but understanding that they exist is the first step toward overcoming them.

Instability

A smaller volume of water is far less stable than a larger volume in terms of its temperature, pH, specific gravity, etc. Changes for the worse occur much more rapidly in a nano tank than they do in a larger system. If the ambient air temperature shifts markedly upward or downward, the water temperature in a smaller volume of water will change much more rapidly than it will in a larger volume of water. Compare the respective cooling rates of a cup of coffee and a pot of hot water and you'll get the general idea.

Water Quality

A modest amount of evaporation results in a significant increase in specific gravity in a smaller system. So forgetting to perform a freshwater top-off—even for one day—could cause a precipitous rise in specific gravity and have a very adverse effect on the well-being of the livestock in a nano system.

Additionally, any contaminants, such as soap or lotion on your hands, that are accidentally introduced or additives that are accidentally overdosed are much more concentrated in a smaller volume of water than they are in a larger volume.

Many of the pomacentrids are good candidates for reef systems, being relatively small fish that won't eat corals, anemones, or other desirable invertebrates.

Lack of Space

Furthermore, the smaller the aquarium, the easier it is to overstock or stock inappropriately. Giving in to the impulse to add "just one more specimen" can tax the biofilter in a system of any size, but in a small system, yielding to this temptation can have a disastrous impact on water quality.

Also, you have to factor in the relative aggressiveness of many pomacentrids when considering keeping them with other species or conspecifics in very confined spaces. If an aggressive damsel or clownfish takes issue with one of its tankmates (or vice versa) in a 100-gallon aquarium, the two can usually stay out of each other's way, thereby minimizing territorial squabbles. But throw the two adversaries together in a 20-gallon tank and they'll fight like two cats in a duffel bag because there's simply no way for each to escape the other's line of sight.

Again, this isn't an attempt to dissuade you from keeping a clownfish or damsel in a smaller system (with the exception of really small nanos, which I would discourage), just to apprise you of the limitations of small systems and the special challenges they present.

Just Right for Reef Tanks

Corals and other sessile invertebrates are the priority in any reef aquarium. The number of fishes is often kept low in order to minimize their impact on water quality, which must be topnotch in a reef system, and any fish specimens that are introduced are chosen for their compatibility with the invertebrates—i.e., they don't include sessile invertebrates as part of their natural menu and they aren't heavy polluters. Many clownfishes and damselfishes satisfy these reef-compatibility requirements superbly, being generally small in size, producing minimal waste, and usually being inoffensive to sessile invertebrates.

Of course, there are exceptions to every rule. For example, the big lip damsel, *Cheiloprion labiatus,* would not be a good candidate for a reef system containing *Acropora* spp., as it feeds primarily on the polyps of those corals. For another, the bowtie or black damsel, *Neoglyphidodon melas,* can't be trusted in a reef system stocked with soft corals, as they compose its natural diet. But most of the commonly sold pomacentrids are generalized omnivores that can be trusted around corals and other sessile invertebrates. If you do your homework by researching the needs of any clownfish or damselfish specimen before you bring it home, you should have no problems in this regard.

All clownfishes are reef-safe in the sense that they won't nip at or eat polyps;

The bowtie damsel is one of the species not safe for reef tanks because they will eat soft corals. This is a juvenile; the adults are solid black in color.

however, as we've already touched upon, they may irritate sessile invertebrates that they've adopted as surrogate hosts, preventing them from expanding their tissues to receive the light they need to sustain themselves. In some cases this can prove deadly to the invertebrate, so if this behavior is observed and it continues unabated, the offending clownfish will need to be removed from the reef system.

Aquascaping the Pomacentrid Aquarium

Whereas some reef fishes demand ample open space for swimming in an aquarium, clownfishes and damselfishes seem to do best when they have lots of structure in which to take refuge. Clownfishes, absent a host anemone or suitable surrogate, will often adopt a small cave or ledge as a safe retreat. Hence a tank containing pomacentrids should be aquascaped to provide lots of nooks, crannies, crevices, and caves.

Gnarled porous live rock is the ideal choice of aquascaping material, as you can stack it in a greater variety of configurations than you can slab-like rocks. You can also join these live rocks together with plastic cable ties or aquarium-safe epoxy or silicone to enhance stability or to create more elaborate aquascaping—such as bridges or overhanging ledges.

Artificial branching stony corals would provide a nice naturalistic setting for species that naturally seek refuge among coral heads, such as the popular humbug damsel, *Dascyllus aruanus,* and its very similarly patterned cousin, the black-tailed humbug, *Dascyllus melanurus.*

As far as substrate goes, crushed aragonite or crushed coral is just fine for pomacentrids. Clownfishes and damsels aren't burrowers, so it's not necessary to provide them with a deep sand bed (DSB) unless you plan to utilize one for the combined purpose of nitrification and natural nitrate reduction. A substrate depth of 2 inches (5 cm) is more than adequate if you just want the tank to have a naturalistic look. For a DSB, a minimum depth of 4 inches (10 cm) is recommended.

For easier maintenance and to minimize the amount of debris that gets trapped in the substrate, where it can decompose and quickly foul the water, many hobbyists who keep nano systems prefer to use no substrate whatsoever. Or, if they want the naturalistic appearance of a crushed aragonite or coral substrate, they might choose to use a faux substrate by gluing a fine layer of substrate material either to the bottom of the tank or to a sheet of glass or acrylic that has been cut to fit the bottom of the tank.

4

Diet and Feeding for Clownfish and Damelfish

The majority of pomacentrids that you're likely to encounter are omnivorous. In nature, some, such as the gregories (*Stegastes* spp.), have a diet that includes a greater proportion of algae, while others, such as the various *Chromis* species, rely more heavily on zooplankton. But few pomacentrids are so specialized in their diet that they completely exclude meat or veggies. That's great news for hobbyists because, as you might expect, fishes that have a generalized diet typically adapt better to aquarium fare and have a much better survival rate in captivity compared to specialized feeders.

The pomacentrids in general are enthusiastic opportunistic feeders. Offer yours a wide variety of foods.

Variety Is the Spice of Life

So, being omnivores, pomacentrids should be offered a diet that is not exclusively plant-based or exclusively protein-based. This is very easy to do nowadays, as the selection of fresh, frozen, dry, and freeze-dried aquarium foods available to hobbyists has never been better.

Your pomacentrid menu should include items such as a staple pellet or flake, spirulina pellets or flakes, frozen mysid shrimp, frozen formulas for both omnivores and herbivores, and, at least occasionally, fresh meaty foods of marine origin, such as clams, shrimp, scallops, and fish, chopped to fit the mouths of pomacentrids.

Crazy Over Clams

Though it's the rare pomacentrid that won't start feeding shortly after purchase, it can sometimes take a day or two to get some specimens interested in eating. This is nothing compared to some marine fishes, such as certain butterflyfishes, which may take several days or even a week or more of coaxing with foods of all sorts before they'll deign to accept anything you offer, but, nonetheless, it can be disconcerting when a clownfish or damselfish ignores your offerings. In such cases you can almost always win over a picky pomacentrid with chopped fresh clams. In fact, there's just something about the scent of fresh clam in the water that really rings the dinner bell for almost any marine fish.

Shucking the fresh clams and chopping the meat is a bit labor-intensive, but you'll find that it's well worth the effort. Make sure the clams you purchase are still alive. Choose only those with their shells clamped tightly shut. Skip any that have gaping shells or an off odor, as they are either dead or dying. I usually buy a large quantity of clams, shuck and chop them all at once, set some of the fresh meat aside in the refrigerator to feed over the course of a few days, and freeze the rest for future use.

I prefer to freeze chopped clams in serving-size batches, so I usually dole out equal-

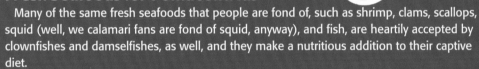

Fresh Seafoods for Pomacentrids

Many of the same fresh seafoods that people are fond of, such as shrimp, clams, scallops, squid (well, we calamari fans are fond of squid, anyway), and fish, are heartily accepted by clownfishes and damselfishes, as well, and they make a nutritious addition to their captive diet.

Whereas a large, predatory fish, such as a lionfish or grouper, can easily consume a whole table shrimp or shucked clam in one gulp, a little bit of these seafoods will go a long way when feeding pomacentrids. Your best bet is to purchase these items in small quantities or set aside a few pieces before preparing your own seafood feast.

Of course, before any of the meaty items mentioned above can be fed to pomacentrids, they must be chopped into pieces small enough to fit their little mouths. This can sometimes be difficult to achieve with a knife because what looks like a tiny piece on the cutting board often proves to be much larger than it appeared after you drop it in the aquarium. A food processor will reduce seafoods to bite-size pieces much more efficiently without making such a mess on your kitchen counter. You can also chop up several different seafoods together for a varied, nutritious blend.

After processing the fresh seafood into tiny pieces, you can set some aside in the fridge to be fed over the next few days. However, whatever won't be fed to the fish within a day or two should be frozen to prevent spoilage. I find it convenient to divide the processed seafood among the compartments of a small ice cube tray, placing just enough for a single feeding in each compartment. That way, I can just pop out a single serving and thaw it out for feeding whenever I need it.

Accounting for Differing Damsel Tastes

Though most pomacentrids are generalized omnivores, eating both meaty and algae-based foods, there are some species that lean more heavily toward the carnivorous or the herbivorous. Examples of the former group include various *Dascyllus* and *Chromis* species, which feed predominately on zooplankton, and representatives of the latter group would include the various algae-farming damsels of the *Stegastes* and *Dischistodus* genera

Most of the fishes in these genera will thrive in captivity if provided an omnivorous diet, but their menu should include a higher proportion of their preferred food items. For example, the domino damselfish, *Dascyllus trimaculatus*, will thrive on regular offerings of small meaty foods, such as frozen mysid shrimp or finely chopped seafoods, supplemented with frozen herbivore formula, shredded sushi nori (or other dried marine algae), and spirulina flakes or pellets. On the other hand, the more herbivorous Beaugregory, *Stegastes leucostictus*, would require a steady ration of herbivore formula, sushi nori, and spirulina supplemented with small meaty foods.

sized portions of the meat into an ice-cube tray. That way, whenever I want to offer my fish a nutritious treat I simply pop one of the servings out of the tray, thaw it, drop the bits into the tank, and watch the fish go crazy!

Cyclops for Small Mouths

A great food to use when trying to elicit an initial feeding response from smaller pomacentrids, especially those that feed on tiny zooplankton in nature, is frozen cyclops. Cyclops is a popular item for feeding sessile invertebrates in reef systems, but I've found that most pomacentrids can't resist them either.

When feeding very small foods such as cyclops, it's helpful to temporarily shut down your filtration and water pumps so there is no water movement. It doesn't take much force to suck these tiny crustaceans into a sump overflow or filter intake or to scatter them all around the aquarium so the fishes never even notice them. But if they are concentrated in one area and allowed to sink slowly to the bottom, they'll get the attention of your fishes and it won't take long for them to start snicking up these minuscule morsels. A little goes a long way when you're using cyclops, so be careful not to overdo it!

Incidental Veggies

If your clownfish or damsel happens to share an aquarium with a herbivorous fish, such as a tang or rabbitfish, there's an easy way to make sure your pomacentrid gets its greens. That is, provide the tang or rabbitfish with a sheet of dried marine algae, such as sushi nori or red or brown marine algae, to nibble on each day. Pomacentrids generally won't tear algae off the sheet, but they will gladly snap up the tiny bits that float around in the water column after the tang or rabbitfish rips into the sheet.

Tasty Tidbits Crawling in the Tank

Though it's not necessary to feed live foods to pomacentrids, they will certainly appreciate and benefit from eating them, and there are various ways—short of actively culturing them or buying them in small, cost-ineffective batches from your local dealer—to provide an ongoing supply of nutritious live foods that your clownfish or damselfish can nibble on.

Aquascaping your tank with copious quantities of quality live rock is one way to introduce populations of these edible organisms. As your system matures, all sorts of little critters will hatch out from the rocks, such as pods—amphipods and copepods—various worms, mollusks, and echinoderms, and clownfishes and damselfishes will gladly gobble up many of them.

Installing a live-sand substrate—or seeding a non-live sand bed with a small quantity of live sand to get the populations started—also is a good way to enhance the microfauna in your system..

Live rock provides clowns and damsels with myriad small organisms upon which to browse.

But perhaps the best way to provide a steady supply of live foods for hungry pomacentrids is to connect some form of refugium to your aquarium. A refugium is essentially a vessel that is separate from your main aquarium but shares the same system water (water is drawn from the display tank, flows through the refugium, and is then pumped back into the display tank). A sump or aquarium of any size can be converted for this purpose. You can also choose from the various commercially manufactured hang-on-tank refugia that are available on the market.

As the name suggests, a refugium provides a safe haven, or refuge, for organisms that would be either eaten or harassed in your display tank. These organisms could include the aforementioned amphipods, copepods, and other desired microfauna, as well as fishes or invertebrates that have been injured or are the target of territorial aggression. Because they are isolated from predators and tormentors, organisms kept in the refugium have the opportunity to reproduce more abundantly than they could in the display tank or to recover from tankmate-inflicted injury.

By placing some pieces of quality live rock and/or a bed of live sand in the refugium, you can establish healthy populations of edible microfauna. As these populations grow, some of these little organisms, along with their eggs and larvae, will be carried into the display tank, where the fish can gobble them up. Those that avoid being eaten will help to establish populations in the main tank, thereby increasing the overall biodiversity of the system.

I should add that many hobbyists also grow various forms of macroalgae, such as *Chaetomorpha* spp. (a.k.a. "chaeto") and *Gracilaria* spp., in their refugia for the purpose of nutrient export. These algae take up dissolved nutrients, such as nitrate and phosphate, from the water, and the aquarist routinely harvests a portion of the algae, thereby removing the nutrients from the system. So, in addition to providing an ongoing smorgasbord of pods, worms, and other tiny critters, a refugium can help to keep your aquarium's water quality at its best.

Many pet stores sell live brine shrimp, and these are but one of a number of live foods you can offer your clowns and damsels.

Mysid Shrimp—Tailor Made for Pomacentrids

Frozen mysid shrimp, *Mysis spp.*, make an ideal staple meaty food for almost all clownfishes and damselfishes. These tiny crustaceans, measuring between ¼ and ½ inch (6 and 12 mm) in total length, are just about the perfect size to fit in the mouths of most adult pomacentrids without the need for chopping, slicing, dicing, or grating. (For juveniles, you might need to start with an even smaller crustacean—frozen cyclops.) Mysids are also a very natural-looking food source that can stimulate a feeding response in even the most finicky fishes.

Furthermore, mysids beat frozen brine shrimp hands down when it comes to nutritional value. Whereas brine shrimp lose almost all of their nutritional value by the time they reach adulthood (unless they are enriched by feeding with a vitamin/fatty acid supplement), adult mysids are high in nutritious protein and fat, making them a perfect complement to herbivorous offerings for omnivorous pomacentrids.

Should You Feed Live Foods?

Of course, live foods, such as mysid shrimp and newly hatched and adult brine shrimp (preferably enriched by feeding with a vitamin supplement), will be accepted with gusto by clownfishes and damselfishes and can certainly be offered as an occasional treat. However, with the variety of high-quality prepared fish foods on the market today, it's really not necessary to offer live foods to pomacentrids on a routine basis. An exception must be made if you decide to breed clownfishes, as the larvae must be fed live marine rotifers and newly hatched brine shrimp, but we'll get into that in greater detail in Chapter 8.

Whatever you do, try to avoid getting too lackadaisical in your feeding, for instance by relying too heavily on only one dry or frozen food for your own convenience.

Kicking Up the Nutritional Value of Your Pomacentrid's Repast

Offering a varied diet is the best way to ensure that your clownfish or damselfish isn't missing an important element in its diet, but as added insurance against dietary deficiencies it's a good idea to occasionally enrich your pomacentrid's food with a nutritional supplement.

Soaking dry or frozen foods with one of the liquid supplements that are available on the market (most contain important vitamins and highly unsaturated fatty acids, or HUFAs) prior to feeding them to your fishes will help to enhance the nutritional value of the foods, which, in turn, will keep your fishes healthier, more colorful, and better able to recuperate from injury or illness. These products can also be fed to live foods—such as brine shrimp—in order to enhance their nutritional value by adding them directly to the water in the culture container.

How Much and How Often

Some reef fishes, including predators like groupers and moray eels, take in large, calorie-dense prey items at a single feeding and can go several days without feeding in between meals. Others can get by perfectly well on once-daily feedings. Still others do best when given several small feedings each day. The clownfishes and damselfishes definitely fall into this last category. They should be offered two or three daily feedings that are small enough to be consumed completely in just a few minutes. Any food that remains uneaten should be vacuumed or netted out so that it doesn't have a chance to decompose and foul your water.

Keep Your Dry Food Fresh

This might sound like a contradiction in terms, but it really is important to make sure you're offering the freshest possible dry foods to your clownfish or damsel. By "fresh" dry food, I mean one that has neither exceeded its expiration date nor been left sitting out exposed to the air for a prolonged period. Remember, the quality and nutritional value of dry flakes and pellets tend to degrade over time and with

Feed your clowns and damsels two or three times daily.

exposure to humidity. Think of it like breakfast cereal. Which box would you rather fill your bowl from in the morning: the one you just purchased and opened within the last few days or the half-empty box that's been languishing in the back of your pantry for the past six months? Not much of a contest, right?

When it comes to flakes, pellets, and other dried foods, it's generally best to buy them in small containers so that the product will be used up completely before it reaches its expiration date. Using it up even sooner would be better. So unless you are feeding a large number of fishes, that value-sized container of marine flake food may not be your best option, as it will have lost much of its quality before you've used up half of it.

A Note on Thawing Frozen Fish Foods

Thawing frozen meaty fish foods invariably yields a certain amount of packing juice in addition to the meat. Introducing this liquid to your aquarium when feeding is not a very good idea. The fish cannot eat it, so it simply adds to the level of dissolved pollutants in your water. As any experienced hobbyist knows, excessive dissolved pollutants can overtax your biological filter as they decompose, and they serve as a fertilizer for undesirable algae.

Your best bet when feeding frozen foods is to place the cube or piece in a fish net and rinse it under cold running tap water until it has thawed completely, or you can swirl it in a small volume of aquarium water and then strain the meat through a fish net over the sink. With either method, all the undesirable liquid will end up going down the drain instead of into your aquarium. The only time this technique isn't recommended is when you're thawing very small frozen foods or certain frozen formula foods that contain tiny ingredients, such as frozen cyclops or very finely chopped greens. In these cases, you're better off placing the portion in a small bowl or cup and thawing it in your refrigerator, since rinsing in a net would result in much, or all, of the product that you paid for being washed down the drain.

In addition to the convenience and variety they offer, another great advantages of frozen foods is that they maintain their quality and nutritional value for a very long time. However, avoid thawing and then refreezing these foods. Much of their nutritional value will be lost as a result, and the food might spoil, which could make your fishes sick.

Pomacentrid Husbandry and Health Care

So now you know how to choose the healthiest clownfish or damselfish at your local fish store, how to provide a menu of nutritious foods to satisfy its omnivorous appetite, and the type of aquarium setup that will best suit your specimen. While those elements fill in a big part of the picture, you must also give some thought to the specific conditions you will be providing in your aquarium—the environment your pomacentrid will soon call home. This chapter will address the subject of appropriate water parameters for pomacentrids as well as some of the healthcare issues you might encounter with that family of fishes.

When keeping your clowns and damsels in a reef tank, keep the specific gravity between 1.024 and 1.025 to ensure that the invertebrates stay healthy.

Standard Marine Water Chemistry Suits Them Fine!

Whereas wild freshwater fishes vary considerably in their water-chemistry needs depending on where in the world they are found, most of the marine fishes sold on the aquarium market are collected from waters with remarkably similar water chemistry (one noteworthy exception would be fishes collected from the Red Sea, which hail from waters with a higher salinity than is typical of other collection sites around the world). Hence, marine fishes collected from, say, Indo-Pacific coral reefs and those collected from tropical Atlantic coral reefs will thrive in waters of identical chemical composition.

As a general rule, clownfishes and damselfishes will do just fine when provided what I would consider standard marine aquarium water chemistry—specific gravity in the range of 1.020 to 1.025, temperature between 75° and 80°F (24° and 27°C), pH of 8.2 to 8.4, alkalinity in the range of 7 to 10dKH (2.5 to 3.5meq/l), and a calcium level between 400 and 450 ppm.

When keeping pomacentrids in a reef or FOWLR (fish-only with live rock) system, or if you're keeping damsels collected from the Red Sea, it's recommended to maintain the specific gravity close to the higher end of the range—1.024 to 1.025. In reef or FOWLR tanks, this isn't for the sake of the clownfishes or damselfishes, but for the invertebrates in the system, which aren't as adaptable as fishes are to variable water parameters. In a fish-only system (i.e., one without live rock and/or sessile invertebrates), non-Red-Sea-collected pomacentrids can be kept with no problem at the lower end of the specific gravity range.

Strive for Stability

Clownfishes and damselfishes are better able to tolerate unstable water parameters than many other marine fishes are, but just because they can tolerate fluctuating conditions—such as tumultuous temperatures, unpredictable pH, and swinging specific gravity—doesn't mean they should be subjected to them. In common with any other fishes collected from a coral-reef environment—one of the world's most stable environments—pomacentrids do best when water conditions are kept as constant as possible. In fact, when it comes to marine aquarium water parameters, it's more critical to maintain a stable value within the recommended range, or even slightly outside the recommended range, than to strive for some arbitrary exact value within the range.

For example, it will be much better for your fishes if you maintain a constant temperature of 81° or 82°F (28°C), which is slightly above the recommended temperature range, than to have a thermometer reading of 80°F (27°C) on one day, 75° (24°C) the next, and 78°(26°C) the day after that. Sure, all those readings fall within the appropriate temperature range for a marine aquarium, but the fluctuations can be very stressful to fishes.

Drip Acclimation: Slow and Steady 'Til Your Fish Is Ready!

It's virtually a given that the water your pomacentrid was kept in at the aquarium store will differ markedly in temperature, pH, specific gravity, and other parameters from the water in your aquarium. For example, most dealers keep the specific gravity in their fish tanks unnaturally low—often as low as 1.017 to 1.018. This is done partly to cut costs by reducing the amount of sea salt mix that is used, but also to reduce the external parasite load on the fishes; whereas the fishes can acclimate readily to the lower specific gravity, many external parasites will be killed by the osmotic shock. Therefore it's critical to acclimate your specimen very slowly to the conditions in its new home. This is best accomplished not by the traditional technique of floating the fish's bag in the quarantine aquarium to equalize the temperature but by a gradual drip-acclimation process to equalize all the water parameters.

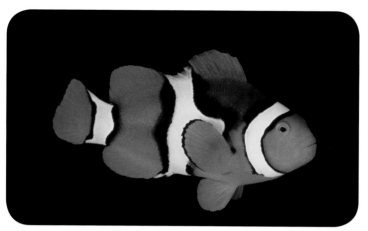

Acclimate your new clown or damsel to the water conditions in your aquarium slowly so that the fish will have time to adapt with minimal stress.

Materials Needed

For this procedure, the only equipment you'll need is a length of flexible airline tubing and a plastic bowl, bucket, or other rigid plastic container. Make sure the tubing is long enough to extend from the top of the aquarium to the bucket or bowl with a little length to spare. The container should be large enough to accommodate at least twice the volume of water in the fish's bag but small enough in diameter across the bottom so that the fish remains fully submerged when it is initially placed into the container along with its shipping water.

Get Dripping!

Once you've assembled your materials, tie two or three loose knots along the length of the airline tubing. (As an alternative, you can use a plastic airline valve to control the flow through the tubing.) Place one end of the tubing in the aquarium (you'll probably need to secure it in place by resting an edge of the aquarium cover on top of it), and extend the other end down to your acclimation container. Gently pour the fish along with its shipping water into the container. Your clownfish or damselfish will be more than a bit skittish and prone to jumping throughout this process, so it's a good idea to place some sort of cover over the container while the fish is acclimating. A towel draped over the top works well.

Next, start the water flowing through the airline tubing. There are three ways you can do this:

1. Suck on the lower end of the tubing until the water gets flowing.
2. Place the top end of the tubing into the return flow of a power filter or the discharge of a powerhead, keeping it under water. When the flow starts through the tubing, fasten it

in the quarantine tank so that it won't pop out of the water.

3. Submerge the entire length of the tubing in the aquarium, maneuvering it to get out all the bubbles and fill it with water. Hold one end in the water, put your finger over the other end, and lower that end to the acclimation container. Release your finger and the flow should begin.

I recommend the last two options, since they never result in a mouthful of yucky aquarium water.

Once the water gets flowing, tighten the knots (or adjust the valve) in the airline tubing until the flow is restricted to a slow, steady drip—one or two drops per second.

Don't Rush It!

Let the water drip until the volume of water in the acclimation container doubles, drain out half of the water and resume dripping until the water volume doubles again. Keep repeating this process—dripping and draining—until the water parameters in your acclimation container match those of your aquarium. It's a good idea to prepare extra salt water ahead of time so you can top off the water that is dripping from your aquarium during the acclimation procedure as needed.

Always place a new fish in a quarantine tank for about four weeks before introducing it to your display aquarium.

Don't Cross Contaminate!

Hobbyists often forget that nasty pathogens and parasites can be transferred from an infected tank to a non-infected tank via aquarium tools, equipment, and buckets, thereby defeating the purpose of quarantining new specimens in the first place. For example, if you have a sick fish in quarantine and you use the same aquarium tongs, fish net, siphon, or test probe in both your quarantine and display tanks, there's a possibility that whatever pathogen or parasite is infecting your quarantined fish will be transferred to your display tank, creating a much bigger healthcare problem than you started with. It's the wise hobbyist who maintains two sets of tools—one set designated for use in the quarantine/hospital tank and the other for use in the display tank. At the very least, tools used for more than one system must be disinfected in between uses.

Commercial disinfecting solutions are available for this purpose, or you can soak the tools in a 10% solution of household bleach and water for about 10 minutes. After the disinfecting soak, rinse the tools thoroughly in tap water to remove all traces of bleach.

Also, to make sure the water dripping from your aquarium mixes properly with the water in the acclimation container—and to ensure that you're getting accurate measurements of specific gravity, temperature, and other parameters—you'll need to stir the water in the container periodically. I've found that using a turkey baster to gently draw in and squirt out water several times at regular intervals gets the job done pretty well.

Once the parameters match, it's safe to release your pomacentrid into the aquarium. However, you don't want to pour the water from the acclimation container into your aquarium. Remember, it contains shipping water from your dealer's tank, which could harbor parasites and, at the very least, is pretty heavily polluted with the specimen's wastes at this point. Instead, use a net to transfer the fish to the aquarium, then dump the water from the acclimation container down the drain.

Drip acclimation can take several hours to complete, and that's a good thing because your fish will adjust to their new living conditions with much less stress when they are acclimated in a slow, steady fashion.

No Pomacentrid Should Be Kept Without Quarantine!

One important point of clarification on the preceding section: when you bring your new clownfish or damselfish home from the fish store, the first aquarium you acclimate it to should not be your main display tank.

With no ifs, ands, or buts, your pomacentrid's first destination should be a quarantine tank, and it should remain there for a minimum of four weeks before you introduce it to your display tank. Period. End of story. Skip this step at your own—and your fish's—peril! If this admonition sounds dire, good! That means I've created the right impression!

Why am I making such a big deal out of quarantine? Let's just say I've paid the price in the past for taking a lackadaisical approach to this vital procedure and there's no reason anyone should have to repeat my mistakes when a quarantine tank is so easy and inexpensive to set up—especially for smaller fishes like pomacentrids.

Why Quarantine?

A four-week quarantine period serves several important purposes. The most obvious is that it gives the hobbyist an opportunity to observe the specimen for evidence of disease or parasites. Trust me when I say that it's infinitely better to find out a fish is sick while it is in isolation than to make this discovery after you've introduced the specimen to your display tank and infected the rest of your fish, possibly wiping out an entire community of valued (and costly) specimens.

But wait a minute. Didn't Chapter 3 cover in detail what to look for in a healthy pomacentrid? If you follow that protocol, why would you end up with a sick clownfish or damselfish to begin with? Well, observing a fish for physical or behavioral symptoms of disease is helpful in weeding out obviously infected specimens, but oftentimes a disease won't become apparent until several days after a fish has been exposed. Hence a perfectly healthy-looking specimen may be a ticking time bomb of illness just waiting to go off in your display tank.

Besides, if you do discover that your new clownfish or damselfish is ill, a quarantine tank is the ideal place to implement a treatment regimen or administer medications. On the other hand, treating a sick fish in a display tank is almost always a bad idea. Why? Consider the following:

- Drugs that are formulated to kill the bad guys (the pathogen you're trying to eradicate) may also kill the good guys (the bacterial colonies that compose your display aquarium's biological filter). So now you've got two problems on your hands rather than one: a tank full of sick fishes and a compromised biofilter.
- It's much less complicated and costly to administer treatments in the smaller volume of water of a quarantine tank than in the larger volume of water in a display tank. It takes ten times as much of a medication to maintain a therapeutic level in a 100-gallon

(400-liter) display tank as it would take to maintain that same level in a 10-gallon (40) quarantine tank.

- Some medications or treatment regimens involve steps such as raising the aquarium temperature or dramatically lowering specific gravity (hyposalinity). These steps are much easier to implement in a small quarantine tank.
- The corals and other sessile invertebrates in reef systems as well as any invertebrates encrusting live rock are very sensitive to medications, especially copper, and to therapies such as hyposalinity. Therefore it is highly problematic to medicate or otherwise treat a sick fish in a reef or FOWLR system.
- It's much easier to monitor a sick fish's recovery or healing process in a small quarantine tank than in a larger display tank where it has numerous places to conceal itself.
- Substrates like coral sand—and even aquarium glass—can take up medications such as copper, creating toxic copper concentrations that preclude the use of this equipment in housing invertebrates from then on.

In addition to its role in disease prevention and treatment, a quarantine tank is the perfect setting in which to introduce a new specimen to the foods you will be offering—and to make sure it's eating them—before it has to compete with other fishes at feeding time. Furthermore, if after quarantine your clownfish or damsel behaves in an overly aggressive manner toward one of its tankmates or becomes the target of another fish's aggression, the aggressor or victim in either case can be transferred immediately to the quarantine tank in order to put an end to hostilities or allow an injured specimen to recover.

A multi-tank quarantine system is fairly inexpensive to set up, although most aquarists probably need just one or two quarantine tanks.

Quarantine Tank Setup

When it comes to quarantine tanks, simpler is definitely better. All you need is a small tank, a 5-gallon (20-liter) or 10-gallon

(100-liter) is fine (even one of those inexpensive plastic aquariums with a slotted lid would suffice for smaller pomacentrids); a heater; a sponge filter or small hang-on filter; a few appropriately sized sections of PVC piping for hiding places; and a cover to keep the fish from jumping out.

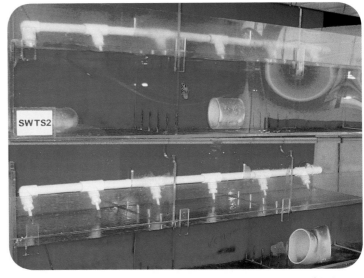

A quarantine tank needs only a minimum of equipment. This is a bare-bones commerical system that has separate compartments for individual specimens.

A light fixture is not absolutely essential, but it is helpful to have some sort of light that you can place over the tank, at least temporarily, so any signs of disease—small white spots, velvety coating, etc.—will be more plainly visible. Symptoms such as these can be hard to see under dim lighting.

A substrate is neither necessary nor, in my opinion, desirable in a quarantine tank, as it can trap debris that will decompose and quickly foul the water in such a small system as well as harbor the cysts of certain parasites. A bare-bottomed tank, on the other hand, can be easily vacuumed to eliminate detritus and cysts.

A few pieces of live rock can be placed in the quarantine tank to provide biological filtration, but keep in mind that the live rock must be removed if treatment with medication becomes necessary. There are two reasons for this. The first is that, as mentioned earlier, the bacteria and invertebrates encrusting the live rock may not be able to tolerate exposure to the medication. The second reason is that, as I pointed out above, certain medications, specifically copper-based ones, will bond chemically with calcareous materials such as live rock and various substrate materials (another reason to avoid the use of a substrate in quarantine), thereby rendering the medication ineffective.

Sterilizing a Contaminated Quarantine Tank

For various reasons, hobbyists may choose to break down and sterilize a quarantine tank after one specimen has been transferred out and before another is introduced. This can be done strictly as a precautionary measure even if the former occupant showed no signs of disease. Why sterilize the tank in that case? It's possible for disease-causing agents to be present in a quarantine system and affect some specimens without affecting others. For example, whereas a healthy, relatively non-stressed, and generally disease-resistant specimen might be able to fight off any infective microbes in the system and, hence, make it through quarantine without exhibiting illness, a specimen that is stressed, malnourished, injured, or otherwise immuno-compromised is far more vulnerable to infection—just as two people can be exposed to the same cold virus with only one (likely the sleep-deprived, overworked one) getting the sniffles.

Of course, tank sterilization is also a good idea in situations where a quarantined specimen was obviously ill and had to be treated or, worse, actually perished in the quarantine tank. In either case, you'd obviously want to make sure that the tank is completely disease-free before introducing another specimen.

To sterilize the tank, simply fill it with a bleach-water mixture at a rate of approximately one cup of bleach per gallon of water (70 ml of bleach per liter of water) and allow it to sit for approximately 10 minutes. Then, drain the tank, rinse it repeatedly with fresh water. If weather allows, this is a job best accomplished outdoors with a garden hose. After rinsing, fill the tank once again with fresh water and treat the water with a chemical dechlorinator to make sure all traces of the bleach have been neutralized. Finally, allow the tank to dry completely.

In addition to the tank, any inert objects or equipment in the system should be sterilized with bleach water and rinsed thoroughly in fresh water, as well. Mechanical filtration media, such as sponges, nylon floss, or power filter cartridges, should be replaced with fresh media.

From Quarantine to Display Tank

Once your clownfish or damselfish has completed a four-week quarantine period without showing any signs of disease and it has learned to accept whatever foods you will be offering, it's ready to graduate to your display tank. At this point, you'll need to acclimate the specimen again—this time to the water in your display tank—via the same drip-acclimation process described above.

It may be tempting to skip this second acclimation process based on the assumption that water conditions in the display tank are likely similar to those of the quarantine tank, but why take chances? In all likelihood, there's at least a modest difference between the two systems. Even if temperature, specific gravity, and pH are virtually identical, there may be a sufficient difference in the level of nitrate or other dissolved pollutants to stress your fish if you introduce it too suddenly.

In the event that your clownfish or damselfish manifests symptoms of disease at any point during the quarantine period, plan to keep it in quarantine for significantly longer than the four-week minimum. In this case you will need to factor in whatever amount of time it takes to effect a cure—i.e., symptoms are no longer present—and then allow for an additional four weeks in quarantine after the last symptoms are seen to ensure that the symptoms don't recur. This requires considerable patience on the hobbyist's part, but there's really no getting around it.

But First, a Freshwater Dip

One very simple, inexpensive, but too often underutilized measure that hobbyists can use to reduce the likelihood of introducing external parasites into their quarantine or display tank is the freshwater dip. Just as it sounds, a freshwater dip involves briefly dipping newly acquired fishes in fresh water before putting them in quarantine (I dip fishes again before moving them to the display tank as well just to be on the safe side).

How will dipping your clownfish or damselfish in fresh water help prevent certain parasites from getting into your aquarium? To understand that, it helps if you understand the concept of osmosis. As you might recall from junior high science class, water will flow from an area of lower solute concentration across a semipermeable membrane to an area of higher solute concentration. When you immerse a saltwater fish harboring external parasites into fresh water, the solute concentration in the fresh water will be significantly lower than the solute concentration within the cells of the parasite. Water therefore will flow into the cells of the parasite, causing them to rupture, thereby killing the parasite. The fish, on the other hand, can generally tolerate the short period in fresh water with no ill effects whatsoever.

First, fill a container with dechlorinated fresh water that has been adjusted to the same temperature and is buffered to the same pH as the water your fish is in. You don't need an especially large container. For most clownfishes or damselfishes, a bowl will usually suffice.

For the most part, pomacentrids are disease-resistant marine fish.

Next, net the fish and submerge it in the fresh water for a period of five to ten minutes. The fish will likely become agitated initially and may struggle a bit or attempt to jump out, so it's a good idea to cover the container during the dip. I use a small piece of transparent acrylic for this purpose because it prevents jumping yet allows me to observe the specimen closely to make sure it's doing okay. In most cases, the fish will soon settle down and become less agitated. The specimen may also lean over onto its side. This is a normal response and nothing to be alarmed about. Throughout the dipping process, watch the specimen closely and be prepared to return it to salt water immediately if it begins to get overly stressed—e.g., thrashing frantically about.

If your clownfish or damsel is infected with external parasites, you may actually see them swell up and drop off the fish's body. However, parasites attacking the internal organs and those that are embedded deep within the fish's tissues will not be affected by a freshwater dip, so this technique cannot be considered a silver bullet against parasites or a substitute for quarantine.

After the freshwater dip is complete and the fish has been returned to salt water, you may observe some loss of equilibrium in the fish—for example, listing, swimming awkwardly, or bumping into objects in the tank. Though disconcerting to watch, this is temporary and will usually resolve on its own in a very short period.

Clownfish and Damselfish Contagions

Pomacentrids tend to be fairly disease-resistant—at least when compared to the fishes of certain other families of marine fishes, such as the acanthurids (tangs and surgeonfishes), which seem to be disease magnets. There are, however, certain maladies that you may encounter when keeping pomacentrids, so it's helpful to have at least a functional understanding of these diseases. What follows is a description of some the more common ailments affecting pomacentrids as well as some insights into their prevention and treatment.

Cryptocaryon irritans, Saltwater Ich

It's the rare marine fish keeper who doesn't do battle, at one time or another, with *Cryptocaryon irritans*, better known as saltwater ich. Fishes infected with *Cryptocaryon*, which is a ciliated parasitic protozoan, will begin scraping their bodies against the substrate, rocks, and other objects in the tank; trembling or twitching nervously; respiring rapidly; and dashing about the tank. They may also refuse food. Tiny white dots, about the size of a grain of salt, will begin to appear on the fish's fins, gills, and

First, Do No Harm

If your clownfish or damselfish begins to show symptoms of disease, resist the impulse to haphazardly dose the tank with all kinds of medications and tonics in the blind hope that one or another will yield a cure. Remember, aquarium pharmaceuticals may do your ailing fish some good if they are dosed appropriately and in strict accordance with the manufacturer's labeling, but they can do a lot more harm than the disease you're trying to combat if they aren't administered properly. Before using any medication to treat a sick fish, ask yourself the following questions:

• Am I certain that I'm observing disease symptoms rather than natural behavior? Could the problem be related to poor water quality or other environmental factors rather than a pathogen? Have I tested all water parameters to make sure they're in the right range?

• Could the problem be related to inadequate nutrition rather than disease and, therefore, be treatable through an improved diet?

• Can I correctly diagnose the disease on my own or do I need to consult an expert, such as a veterinarian or knowledgeable aquarist?

• Do I have the right medication for the job?

• Would a non-pharmaceutical approach, such as a freshwater dip or hyposalinity, be just as effective or even more effective at treating the problem?

• Will this medication affect my hospital tank's biological filter?

• Have I determined the exact volume of water in the hospital tank, factoring in displacement by rocks and other objects in the tank, for proper dosing?

body. The visible white dots are not the actual parasites. Rather, the dots develop when the fish's body attempts to wall off the parasites by forming cysts around them. If left untreated—and especially if the affected fish are otherwise stressed or malnourished— *Cryptocaryon* can be fatal.

To understand how to prevent or treat an outbreak of *Cryptocaryon*, you must have an understanding of the parasite's somewhat complex lifecycle. You see, the parasite that is attached to and actively feeding on a fish represents only one part of this lifecycle. After feeding on the fish—and driving it crazy—for several days to about a week, the parasites detach from the fish and drop to the substrate. At this point, it might appear as if the fish has gotten better and all is well in the aquarium, but the parasites are simply regrouping to launch a much larger assault later on. That is, after they've dropped to the substrate, each parasite attaches to a surface and forms a cyst. Inside the cyst, the parasite divides into several hundred parasites. This stage can last for as long as a month. Then the cysts hatch and the parasites swarm into the water column looking for a fish host to infect. If they find a fish, the whole cycle repeats itself. However, if no host fish is found, the free-swimming *Cryptocaryon* parasites, which are obligate parasites of fishes (they must parasitize a fish to survive), will die within a day or two.

Copper-based medications can be effective at eradicating *Cryptocaryon* when administered in strict accordance with product labeling; however, copper definitely has its drawbacks—not the least of which is that clownfishes can be sensitive to it. To be effective, copper must be maintained at a very precise level. Too little won't get the job done, and too much can be fatal. Also, copper is lethal to invertebrates, so it must never be used in reef or FOWLR systems.

A much safer technique, and one that I've used to treat *Cryptocaryon* successfully on several occasions, is to keep the fish in quarantine, give the specimen freshwater dips once a day over the course of about a week, and continue to perform massive daily water changes until the symptoms have subsided (repeating a course of freshwater dips if symptoms recur). During each water change, I take care to vacuum the entire tank bottom and rinse off any objects

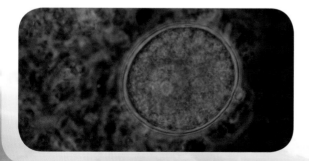

Magnified view of an ich parasite, *Cryptocaryon irritans*.

in the tank in fresh water so that I can eliminate as many cysts and free-swimming parasites as possible.

If this technique isn't successful, you can also try performing a hyposalinity treatment. This involves very gradually lowering the specific gravity in your quarantine tank or fish-only aquarium (never in a reef or FOWLR system) to the range of 1.010-1.012 and keeping the specific gravity in that range for at least four weeks. As when performing a freshwater dip, hyposalinity kills parasites through osmotic shock. The fishes, on the other hand, will be able to tolerate the significantly lower specific gravity provided it is lowered and raised again very gradually.

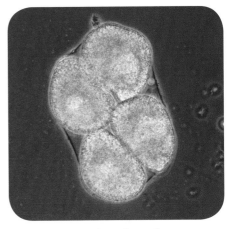

Magnified view of marine velvet, *Amyloodinium ocellatum*

So what happens if you've skipped the vital step of quarantine only to discover that your new clownfish or damselfish has a case of *Cryptocaryon* after you've introduced it to your display tank? Well, the severity of your predicament depends on the size of the community in your aquarium, because if one fish in the system is infected, you must assume all are infected. If you have a lot of fishes in a true fish-only system, you can try to treat them all in place, but this is not ideal if you plan to medicate the tank with copper, as the copper will bond with the calcareous materials in your tank, reducing its efficacy. The copper that has bonded to the rocks or substrate can also be released into the system for many years to come, making the tank unsuitable for invertebrate life in the future—for instance, if you eventually decide to convert your fish-only tank to a FOWLR or reef system. Of course, if you currently have a reef or FOWLR system, your only option is to remove all the fishes to a hospital tank for treatment, as the invertebrates in these systems will not tolerate medications or hyposalinity.

When *Cryptocaryon* is introduced into a reef or FOWLR tank on an infected fish, the obvious challenge becomes finding a way to completely eradicate the parasite from the system, since you're unable to use medications or hyposalinity in such systems. The good news is that there's a very low-tech solution to this problem. Remember, *Cryptocaryon irritans* is an obligate parasite of fishes. Without a fish host present in the aquarium, all of the free-swimming parasites that hatch out will die within a few days. So by transferring all of the fishes from the display tank to a separate quarantine tank for a period of four to six weeks (which you'll need to do in order to treat them, anyway), you'll effectively disrupt the parasite's lifecycle and, ultimately, eradicate it from the tank.

Amyloodinium ocellatum, Marine Velvet

As with fishes infected with *Cryptocaryon irritans*, fishes infected with *Amyloodinium ocellatum*, or marine velvet, often scrape their bodies on objects in the tank, exhibit labored respiration, refuse food, twitch nervously, and dash about the tank. Because *Amyloodinium* parasites tend to affect the gills first, the characteristic physical symptom—a fine velvety or powdery coating on the fish's body—doesn't usually become evident until the later stages of the disease. Unfortunately, at that point the specimen may already be past the point of no return.

Amyloodinium has a lifecycle that is very similar to that of *Cryptocaryon*. However, this parasitic dinoflagellate is far more virulent, progresses through its lifecycle much more rapidly, and is more often fatal to infected specimens. Whereas the encysted reproductive stage of *Cryptocaryon* can last as long as a month, this stage takes less than a week (three to five days) with *Amyloodinium*. Furthermore, the free-swimming, infective stage for *Amyloodinium* is significantly longer than that of *Cryptocaryon*—one to two weeks versus one to two days. In other words, successive waves of infective

Usually, only wild-caught clownfish and damsels carry clownfish disease—another reason to purchase tank-raised fish.

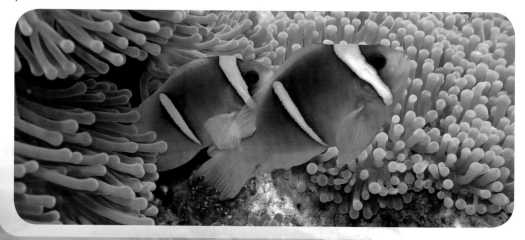

parasites are released into the tank at much closer intervals, and the free-swimming parasites have much more time to find and infect a host fish.

Your best options for treating *Amyloodinium* are hyposalinity and/or copper medication administered in a hospital tank. Given the abbreviated window of opportunity for treating this virulent disease, I would recommend a freshwater dip to remove as many of the parasites as possible before proceeding with hyposalinity or copper treatment. As with *Cryptocaryon*, if you've skipped quarantine and introduced an infected specimen to an established community of fishes, you must assume that all of the fishes are infected and treat them accordingly.

Once *Amyloodinium* has been introduced into a display tank, completely eradicating the parasite will require allowing the tank to run fallow—with no fish present—for four to six weeks.

Brooklynella hostilis, Clownfish Disease

No discussion of diseases affecting pomacentrids would be complete without mention of *Brooklynella hostilis*, better know as clownfish disease. *Brooklynella* is a common disease of wild-caught clownfishes (one more good reason to buy tank-bred clownfishes!). However, contrary to what its common name implies, this parasite is known to infect a variety of non-clownfish species, as well, including (but certainly not limited to) other species of damselfishes.

Like both *Cryptocaryon* and *Amyloodinium*, Brooklynella is a parasitic protozoan. However, it differs significantly from both in that is has a direct lifecycle. That is, the parasites live, feed, and multiply on a host fish, then drop off into the water where they can immediately infect other fishes. There is no intervening dormant reproductive stage.

Infected specimens typically react by producing copious amounts of mucus, which will appear as white patches or a white film on the body. In addition, they'll exhibit faded coloration, rapid breathing and gasping, and loss of appetite.

It's important to be aware that fish infected with *Brooklynella* can succumb to the disease very rapidly. In fact, death can occur within mere hours of symptom onset. That means you must act fast if you hope to save an infected specimen.

The first intervention should be a freshwater dip to reduce the parasitic load on the infected specimen. This will often buy enough time to administer other treatments and may give the fish sufficient relief to encourage it to start eating again. Whereas copper is effective in treating *Cryptocaryon* and *Amyloodinium*, it is not effective against *Brooklynella*. The most commonly recommended medication of choice for treating

Squabbles between tankmates sometimes result in eye injuries. However, if both of a fish's eyes are cloudy or bulging, the culprit is likely a bacterial infection.

Brooklynella is a formalin-based medication (available in various commercial preparations), which should be administered to the fish in daily short-term baths for approximately a week to ten days, in strict accordance with product labeling.

Like *Cryptocaryon* and *Amyloodinium*, *Brooklynella* is an obligate parasite of fish, so the best method for eradicating it from an infected display tank is to remove all fishes from the system and allow it to run fallow for at least a month.

Bulging Or Cloudy Eyes

The symptom of cloudy eyes or bulging eyes (exophthalmia, or pop-eye) on your clownfish or damselfish can result from several potential root causes. In many cases, you can trace these symptoms to a physical injury, perhaps acquired in a territorial dispute with a tankmate or as a result of skittish behavior upon introduction to the confines of a new aquarium. When only one eye is affected, you can usually assume that some type of injury (or bacterial infection secondary to injury) is to blame. Two cloudy or bulging eyes, on the other hand, usually signify a bacterial infection, often resulting from poor water quality. Certain nutritional deficiencies can also manifest themselves through clouding or bulging of the eyes.

If you suspect, or know, that injury was the cause of the eye-bulging or cloudiness, keep watch on the specimen while maintaining impeccable water quality and continuing to offer a varied, nutritious diet. The affected eye should begin to show improvement within a few days. If it doesn't start to improve—or if the cause of the initial injury has not been mitigated (for example, if the affected pomacentrid is still being harassed by a tankmate or behaving in an excessively nervous manner)—it may be necessary to isolate it in your quarantine tank so it has a chance to settle down and recover in peace. Adding Epsom salts to the quarantine tank at a rate of 1 teaspoon per 10 gallons (40 liters) of water will also help to reduce eye swelling.

In the event that both eyes are affected or one eye doesn't improve through isolation and improved husbandry, it may be necessary to medicate the affected fish with antibiotics, following the manufacturer's dosing instructions to the letter. Of course, any antibiotic regimen should be administered in a separate quarantine tank, never in a main display tank. Remember, antibiotics are formulated to kill bacteria, and that means they just might wipe out, in addition to the pathogens you're trying to eradicate, the beneficial nitrifying bacteria that provide your system's biological filtration.

Head and Lateral Line Erosion (HLLE)

Whereas the cause of diseases such as *Cryptocaryon*, *Amyloodinium*, and *Broolynella* are well documented and understood, the cause of head and lateral line erosion, or HLLE, remains something of a mystery—or, at least, a source of contention among experts. Numerous possible explanations have been put forth, including (among others) nutritional deficiencies, poor water quality, stray voltage from faulty electrical equipment, a flagellated protozoan, and the use of activated carbon (thought to either leach something harmful into the water or adsorb something beneficial from the water). What's most interesting about HLLE is that it is not known to affect fishes in

Clownfish Freckles

It's not uncommon for clownfishes kept in reef aquariums to suddenly exhibit little black dots in various locations on their body while they continue to behave and eat perfectly normally. For marine aquarium hobbyists, who are conditioned to view any unusual coloration or spots on a fish as evidence of a parasite or disease, the sudden appearance of these dots can be very upsetting and may send them dashing to the aquarium store to buy a cartload of medications.

But these clownfish freckles are not usually cause for alarm. Oftentimes, these spots are simply a form of hyper-pigmentation brought about by contact with an unnatural host invertebrate—perhaps as a result of exposure to stinging tentacles or to chemicals produced by the invertebrate. Whatever the exact mechanism that produces these spots, they often clear up with no help from the hobbyist once the clownfish acclimates to the surrogate host or stops attempting to take refuge in it.

the wild. In other words, it is strictly a disease of aquarium fishes.

HLLE manifests itself through the appearance of pits, holes, or ulcers on the head and along the lateral line of the affected specimen. The pits often start very small, but they will gradually expand and begin to connect, sometimes resulting in very large areas of tissue loss. These lesions do not bleed and are usually characterized by an absence

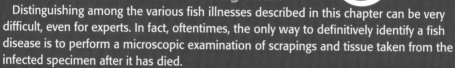

Which Ailment Are You Dealing with?

Distinguishing among the various fish illnesses described in this chapter can be very difficult, even for experts. In fact, oftentimes, the only way to definitively identify a fish disease is to perform a microscopic examination of scrapings and tissue taken from the infected specimen after it has died.

Behavioral symptoms such as body scraping, twitching, and labored respiration can accompany many fish diseases, so observing these symptoms is certainly not diagnostic. Furthermore, similar symptoms can be brought about by certain environmental factors, such as the presence of ammonia, an excessively high nitrate level, or a low dissolved oxygen level.

But what about those "characteristic" outward physical symptoms, such as the presence of little white spots on the fish's body or excessive mucus production? Surely we can rely on those to make an accurate diagnosis. Or, can we?

We know, for example, that *Cryptocaryon irritans* causes little white dots that are about the size of a grain of salt while *Amyloodinium ocellatum* causes much smaller dots that look like powdery patches on the fish's body. But realistically, it's not always such a simple matter for the untrained eye to distinguish between the two—especially in the early stages of the disease when spots may not yet be present or on a fish that is dashing nervously about the tank or attempting to conceal itself.

As for excessive mucus production, while this symptom is commonly exhibited by fish infected with *Brooklynella hostilis*, it can also be caused by a host of other diseases and environmental problems. So this symptom, too, is only part of the diagnostic picture.

So, does all this mean you shouldn't attempt to diagnose and treat a sick fish? Not at all, but it should suggest that it's very important to consider the whole constellation of symptoms—both behavioral and physical—and to rule out the possibility that the problem is environmental in origin before making an educated guess as to which disease you're dealing with and beginning any treatment regimen. If you can enlist the input of a veterinarian or knowledgeable aquarist before making a diagnosis, all the better.

The cause of head and lateral line erosion (show here on a tang, *Zebrosoma* sp.) is poorly understood, but improper aquarium conditions and diet are likely suspects.

of pigment. Hence they tend to appear white or lighter in color than the surrounding healthy tissue. HLLE is a chronic condition that is not immediately life-threatening, but it can lead to death in severe cases. At the very least, the pitting can cause permanent scarring and leaves the specimen vulnerable to secondary infection.

Though the actual cause of HLLE may be subject to debate, the advance of the symptoms can usually be halted—and even reversed if caught early enough—by taking steps to improve the specimen's nutrition and environmental conditions. Make sure you're providing a varied diet of high-quality dry, fresh, and frozen foods. It's also recommended to enrich the foods you offer with a quality supplement containing essential vitamins, lipids, and fatty acids. Vigorous protein skimming and a stepped-up regimen of water changes will help to keep your water conditions in top shape. Stress may play a contributing role in the onset of HLLE, so it's a good idea to eliminate from the equation any potential stressors, such as aggressive tankmates or excessive activity in the vicinity of the aquarium.

Send In the Clowns!

Now it's time to get a little better acquainted with some of the clownfish and damselfish species you might encounter for sale at your local aquarium store—along with a few rare species that you might come across only if you're lucky. We'll start with the clownfishes in this chapter, and then we'll give the damselfishes the same treatment in Chapter 7.

Clark's clownfish is one of the largest clowns and is also fairly aggressive. Keep this species by itself or in mated pairs.

Common Clownfishes

The following clownfish species are very commonly available in the aquarium trade. You're likely to come across many, if not all, of them at any well-stocked retailer specializing in marine fishes, and captive-bred specimens of each are routinely available. Most are also quite hardy and very adaptable to aquarium conditions, especially when captive-bred specimens are chosen.

Captivating Clarks

Amphiprion clarkii, or Clark's clownfish, is one of the most common clownfish species available in the aquarium trade. At over 5 inches (13 cm) in maximum length, it's also among the largest. Furthermore, it's one of the most rugged of the clownfishes—indeed, one of the most rugged aquarium fishes in general—and is a good choice for hobbyists making their first foray into saltwater fish-keeping. Even better for hobbyists who are interested in keeping this species, captive-bred specimens of *A. clarkii* are readily available on the market, and they're even more bulletproof than their wild-caught kin!

A. clarkii tends to defy easy physical description, as this species exhibits considerable color variation depending on where it is collected and other factors such as age and sex. This fish is often yellow or brown in base coloration or has a yellow or orange face giving way to brown over the rest of its body. In some cases, however, the yellow or orange coloration extends over a much greater portion of the specimen's body. There's even a melanistic form that is black in base coloration, with a white or yellow face. The tail color of this species is also quite variable, ranging from white to yellow to combinations thereof.

The vertical white body bands on *A. clarkii* are typically broad and bold, with one occurring just behind the eye and another in mid-body. A third, narrow white band is present just in front of the caudal fin of some color forms but absent in others. Or it may be present but indistinguishable in specimens exhibiting a white caudal fin.

One of the more aggressive clownfishes, *A. clarkii* is best kept one specimen to a tank or in mated pairs. Other clownfish species and more passive tankmates may also elicit aggression from *A. clarkii*. Given its rather respectable adult size (as clownfishes go, anyway), *A. clarkii* is not a good choice for a nano aquarium. A tank in the range of 29 to 40 gallons (110 to 160 liters) would be a more appropriate minimum housing for this species.

Tough Tomatoes

The tomato clownfish, *Amphiprion frenatus*, is another extremely hardy (especially when captive-bred), beginner-friendly species that can exceed 5 inches (13 cm) in length. Not a good choice for a nano tank, this species needs plenty of space. A

The tomato clown (left) is a large and hardy clownfish suitable for beginners. The related red saddleback clown (*A. ephippium*, right) is less common in the pet trade but is also a good choice for new clown keepers.

minimum of 29 to 40 gallons (110 to 160 liters) is recommended. *A. frenatus* can become quite cantankerous towards other clownfishes (especially conspecifics) and toward other more passive or similar-looking tankmates, so it is best housed one to a tank or in a mated pair and with equally assertive but dissimilar species.

This species has a reputation for pulling the proverbial Jekyll and Hyde routine—behaving innocuously enough toward its tankmates for some time but then turning into a real bully once it matures. Keep that propensity—and its ultimate size—in mind when selecting fishes to share its tank space.

A. frenatus ranges in color from yellowish-orange to bright red. Females begin to exhibit a dark brown hue along their flanks as they age. The color of the fins matches the overall body color. Juvenile tomato clownfish exhibit three vertical white (or blue in some color variants) bands, one behind the eye, one at mid-body, and one in front of the tail. However, in common with similar clownfish species, as this species ages the mid-body and tail bands fade away, leaving only the head band. As with *A. clarkii*, this species exhibits some color variation depending on the region from which it is collected.

Awesome Ocellaris

The ocellaris clownfish, *Amphiprion ocellaris*, thought by many novice hobbyists or non-hobbyists to be *the* clownfish, is another commonly sold species that is very hardy and well suited for beginners' tanks. However, it's important to make a distinction between wild-caught and captive-bred specimens of *A. ocellaris*. The former have a very poor track record of survival—and, indeed, are best avoided altogether—whereas the latter are about as durable as they come.

Tank-raised ocellaris clowns are very hardy fish, but their wild-caught counterparts tend to fare poorly in the aquarium.

If you want to add this iconic clownfish to your aquarium and see it survive and thrive, do yourself a favor by purchasing a tank-bred specimen. Ocellaris clownfish are routinely bred in captivity and are available anywhere marine fishes are sold. They're also very modestly priced, so there's simply no reason whatsoever to purchase wild-caught specimens.

The percula clown is smaller and more aggressive than the otherwise similar ocellaris clown.

A. ocellaris is bright orange in overall coloration, and it has broad white head, mid-body, and tail bands outlined in black. The center of the mid-body band bulges out in the direction of the fish's head. All of the fins are orange with distinct black margins.

At just over three inches (8 cm) in adult size, *A. ocellaris* is well suited to life in smaller aquariums and is one of the better clownfishes for nano tanks. This species is also one of the more peaceful clownfishes and can even be kept in small conspecific groups in larger systems provided all of the specimens are of similar size and are introduced into the tank at the same time.

Perky Perculas

The percula clownfish, *Amphiprion percula*, is almost identical to the ocellaris clown in appearance. However, *A .percula* stays a bit smaller (in fact, it's among the smallest of the clownfishes), reaching right around 3 inches (8 cm), and the white bands on *A. percula* tend to have a more pronounced black edging. There can also be differences in the number of dorsal spines and dorsal soft rays between these two species, but there is overlap, so that isn't usually definitive.

As far as tank size and general aquarium care are concerned, *A. percula* and *A. ocellaris* have identical requirements. It's also equally well suited to life in the nano tank. Furthermore, the same admonition of buying tank-raised versus wild-caught specimens applies.

Behaviorally, you might notice that *A. percula* is a bit more belligerent toward its own and other species than *A. ocellaris* is, so it's best to keep this species singly or in mated pairs and with tankmates that aren't overly passive or too similar to the clownfish in size or color. And, as I can attest from long personal experience, this species will bite the hand that feeds it, too (recall the description of my hand-biting percula clownfish in Chapter 2).

The Maroon Stands Alone

Premnas biaculeatus, the maroon (or spinecheek) clownfish, is a real standout among the clownfishes for many reasons. It stands alone as the only clownfish out of all 28 species that does not belong to the genus *Amphiprion*.

The largest of the clownfishes, *P. biaculeatus* tops out at over 6 inches (15 cm). This species also exhibits the greatest size disparity between males and females of all the clownfish species, with males reaching only about a third of the size of females. Its large adult size should suggest to potential keepers that a larger tank is in order for *P. biaculeatus*. An aquarium of 40 gallons (160 liters) or more would not be excessive for this species, especially if kept in a pair.

The maroon clownfish is set apart physically from the *Amphiprion* clowns because of the presence of sharp spines on its cheeks. When transferring a maroon clownfish, it's easy to get those cheek spines entangled in a net, making it difficult to

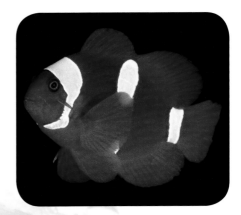

Maroon clownfish are unique in the family for possessing a sharp spine on each cheek.

Pink skunk clowns are skittish fish and should not be kept with larger or more aggressive pomacentrids.

release the fish and potentially causing injury to it, so it's better to herd the specimen into a rigid container for transfer rather than attempting to net it.

Maroon clownfishes are dark orange to red in overall color with narrow white head, mid-body, and tail bands. Specimens collected from reefs around Sumatra exhibit somewhat broader bands that are yellow in color. As female maroon clownfish age, the orange or red coloration changes to a reddish brown.

Yet another characteristic that sets *P. biaculeatus* apart is its renowned aggressiveness. Members of this species—particularly the females—are the real bruisers of the clownfish world. Keeping more than one to a tank is to invite perpetual squabbles. Mated pairs can be kept together, but the smaller male must be provided abundant safe retreats that the larger female cannot access in the event that she gets her ire up and decides to take it out on her mate. When choosing tankmates for *P. biaculeatus*, avoid other clownfishes as well as any species that are more passive in disposition.

A Pink Skunk

Though regularly available in the aquarium trade, the pink skunk clownfish, *Amphiprion perideraion*, differs from the previously discussed common clowns in that it tends to be more skittish and a bit more touchy when it comes to water quality. Hence this species is perhaps not one of the best choices for the novice clownfish keeper. Captive-bred specimens are, however, more predictably durable and adaptable. Also, whereas the other common species described above can be troublemakers when kept with more passive species, *A. perideraion* is more likely to be the target of aggression from more assertive tankmates. Though potentially aggressive toward conspecifics and other similar-looking skunk clowns, this species will usually coexist peacefully with other clownfish species.

As its common name suggests, *A. perideraion* is pink to apricot in overall color with a skunk-like white stripe running from its nose down the length of its back. It also exhibits a narrow vertical white band on its head. This latter feature makes it easy to distinguish *A. perideraion* from the very similar-looking skunk clownfish, *Amphiprion akallopisos,* and the orange skunk clownfish, *Amphiprion sandaracinos*, both of which lack a head band. Maximum size for this species is approximately 4 inches (10 cm), and it should be afforded an aquarium that is, at minimum, in the range of 20 to 29 gallons (75 to 110 liters).

Uncommon clownfishes

What follows is a small sampling of clownfish species that are rare in the aquarium trade and appear with less frequency or predictability than the bread-and-butter clowns we've discussed thus far. This is often attributable to their having a very limited distribution or the fact that they don't tend to withstand the rigors of collection and shipping very well. However, if you keep your eyes open, you might see some of these rare beauties gracing the display tanks at your local fish store from time to time. You may also come across various rare clownfishes for sale through online sources. Of course, you can expect any rare clownfish species to be accompanied by a higher price tag—sometimes significantly higher!

The Seychelles clownfish is uncommon in the aquarium trade and only rarely bred in captivity.

Stunning Seychelles

Hailing from the waters of the Seychelles Islands and Aldabra Atoll in the western Indian Ocean, the Seychelles clownfish, *Amphiprion fuscocaudatus*, is a very comely species that only occasionally makes its way into the aquarium trade. As this species reaches a respectable 5.5 inches (14

Wide-band clownfish hail from less tropical waters than most other species and require cool temperatures in the aquarium.

cm) in total length, its minimal housing requirement is an aquarium in the range of 29 to 40 gallons (110 to 160 liters).

To my knowledge this species is not currently being bred in captivity on any significant scale. Therefore any specimen you should happen to find for sale in your local fish store or online will likely have been wild-collected.

Dark brown in overall color, *A. fuscocaudatus* possesses white head, mid-body, and tail bands that are subtly outlined in blue. Contrasting nicely with the brown hue is a striking shade of yellow occurring on the fish's chin and belly as well as on the pectoral, pelvic, and anal fins. The dorsal and caudal fins are light gray, with charcoal-colored streaks accenting the fin rays. This last feature helps distinguish this species from similarly colored clownfish.

A Truly Cool Clown

The wide-band clownfish, *Amphiprion latezonatus,* is more than just visually distinctive; it also differs in its environmental needs from all the other clownfishes described in this chapter. Whereas most clownfishes thrive in tropical temperatures, *A. latezonatus*, from the waters around the Lord Howe Island group (off eastern Australia) and near Queensland and New South Wales, is one of only two clownfish species that hail from cooler waters (the other is *A. mccullochi*, McCulloch's clownfish), preferring water temperatures in the high 60s to low 70s Fahrenheit (20° to 23°C). On the off chance that you should come across a specimen and choose to purchase it, this temperature requirement would need to be taken into consideration, and you will need a chiller for the aquarium. Also, take heed of the general caution about the touchiness of saddleback clownfishes in the upcoming section on *A. polymnus*.

A. latezonatus reaches approximately 5.5 inches (14 cm) and would require a tank of at least 29 to 40 gallons (110 to 160 liters). It is dark brown in overall color, with white head, mid-body, and tail bands that are tinged with blue. The trailing edge of the caudal fin is white as well. One of its common names, wide-band clownfish, is derived from the broad pyramidal (narrower at the top and wider at the bottom) mid-body band. It's also interesting to note that this species can develop a pale blue tinge on its lips.

A Rare Gem From Oman

Found only off the coast of Oman on the Arabian Peninsula, *Amphiprion omanensis* is extremely rare in the aquarium hobby, and data are scarce on its care requirements, though Michael (2008) reports that it usually does well in captivity.

A. omanensis rivals *P. biaculeatus* in adult size, reaching approximately 6 inches (15 cm) in total length. If you should be fortunate enough to find one of these rare gems, it should be given a tank that is at least 40 gallons (160 liters) in capacity. I would also err on the side of caution by keeping this species one to a tank or in mated pairs and only with non-aggressive tankmates.

The Oman clownfish is orange-brown in overall color and has two very narrow white bands, one on the head and the other at mid-body. Its pelvic and anal fins are dark brown. The tail and caudal peduncle are whitish in color, and the tail is lyre shaped—an unusual clownfish attribute.

Saddleback clowns are skittish and often fail to adapt to the aquarium, so they are best left to experts.

Saddle Up

The saddleback clownfish, *Amphiprion polymnus*, is highly variable in underlying coloration, including various shades of orange, yellow, brown, or even black and various combinations of colors. Its common name is derived from the white saddle-shaped band that originates about halfway up its

What Else Is Hiding Among Anemone Tentacles?

Contrary to popular perception, clownfishes haven't cornered the market when it comes to anemone symbiosis. Other creatures can be found hiding amidst the protective tentacles of sea anemones, as well. For example, many shrimps of the genus *Periclimenes*, the so-called anemone shrimps (see photo on right), depend on a host sea anemone for survival just as clownfishes do.

Perhaps these dainty shrimps don't share the clownfishes' celebrity simply because they can be downright difficult to spot. Many *Periclimenes* species reach the rather unimpressive adult size of approximately 1 inch (2.5 cm). Plus, their bodies are often nearly transparent, giving rise to another common name, glass shrimps. Also, whereas clownfishes will thrive in aquariums without an anemone, the same can't be said for the anemone shrimps. They simply cannot thrive in captivity when no host anemone is present.

sides and extends upward and back through the dorsal fin. This species also has a broad white head band, and its tail is bordered in white. In some color variants, a white band also appears on the caudal peduncle.

Another respectably sized clown, reaching approximately 5 inches (13 cm), this species should be kept in a tank no smaller than 29 gallons (110 liters). Regardless of the size of the tank accommodating it, this is not among the easier clowns to maintain in captivity, often acclimating poorly and behaving skittishly. Wilkerson (2001) describes the three saddleback species as being "perhaps the clownfish group least suited to captivity" and observes that these species are highly prone to panicky behavior when getting acclimated, especially when disturbed at night. She further notes that these fishes "also suffer from collection and transportation stress and often arrive at retailers' shops in poor condition." If you ask me, this sounds like a pretty good argument for leaving these species to the experts or purchasing only captive-bred specimens if you can find them.

7

Damsels, the Delightful and the Dastardly

Whereas it was fairly easy to select a cross-section of clownfish species to introduce in chapter 6 (given the fact that there are only 28 clownfish species in total), it's a much bigger challenge to narrow down a representative sampling of damselfishes. There are just so many beautiful and fascinating damsels to choose from! In this chapter, therefore, I've tried to include descriptions of several common damselfishes that you're likely to encounter at your local fish store as well as a few rare species, but keep in mind that these accounts barely scratch the surface. Still, I hope this chapter piques your interest in the delightful—and occasionally dastardly—damselfishes.

Blue-green chromis live in large schools that hide and forage among the branches of *Acropora* corals.

Aquarium market mainstays

The following damselfish species are fairly ubiquitous in the aquarium trade. Nonetheless, one could justifiably argue that all are exceptional species in their own right.

A Sociable Damsel

The first species we'll look at, the blue-green chromis, *Chromis viridis*, is not only one of the most common damselfishes available in the aquarium trade but also one of the most peaceful damsels. In fact, the best way to keep this schooling species in the aquarium is in a group consisting of six or more specimens. Specimens kept singly usually fare poorly, and smaller groups aren't recommended, because a pecking order may develop, with the more passive specimens receiving the brunt of the bullying. When larger groups are kept, however, any aggression that develops is diffused among a greater number of specimens, so it's less likely that one will be singled out and badgered.

C. viridis is completely inoffensive toward other species, but it can be the target of aggression from more assertive tankmates, so it's important to choose species that are equally passive.

C. viridis reaches approximately 4 inches (10 cm) in length and, as its common name suggests, is iridescent blue-green in color. However, its color can appear quite variable, depending on the specimen's mood and the lighting under which it's kept. In common with all other *Chromis* species, its tail is deeply forked.

Though individuals of this species reach a relatively modest adult size, the fact that they must be kept in groups necessitates a larger aquarium. To house a school of six specimens, a tank in the range of 40 to 55 gallons 160 to 210 liters) would be appropriate. Also, be sure to provide plenty of nooks and crannies for hiding. Because *C. viridis* typically resides among the branches of *Acropora* corals in nature, a reef system containing *Acropora* spp. would be ideal captive housing for this species. Absent live corals, live rock aquascaping with lots of caves and crevices will certainly suffice. You can also employ artificial branching corals to create a naturalistic habitat for this species.

In general, *C. viridis* is a hardy species that is a good choice for novice hobbyists, but this applies only to healthy specimens. Unfortunately, owing to the rigors of capture and prolonged shipping, many specimens arrive on the market in suboptimal condition. It's a good idea to put a hold on any specimens you're thinking of buying for a few days

Although the blue devil damselfish is often hostile to other fish, it ignores most of the invertebrates typically kept in reef systems.

before you take them home to ensure that they're eating and getting acclimated to captivity and that they're not stressed beyond recovery.

The Devil Made Me Do It

Chrysiptera cyanea, the blue devil damselfish, is fairly ubiquitous in the aquarium trade and is often one of the first saltwater fishes kept by novice aquarists. Unfortunately, this species is also frequently used to cycle new aquariums—a deplorable practice that, as we established in Chapter 2, should be shunned in favor of live rock cycling and other fishless cycling techniques.

Though by no means one of the most belligerent damselfishes, *C. cyanea*—especially mature males of the species—will more than live up to its common name in captivity, continuously harassing more peaceful species, even fishes much larger than itself, so choose tankmates with this propensity in mind. Ironically, this devilish species can be housed in groups, provided they are kept one male with several females and/or juveniles or all females and/or juveniles with no males.

But one note of caution when keeping this species in a group, even one consisting of all females: make sure all of the specimens in the group are very similar in size. In situations where several unequally sized individuals are kept together, it can happen that the smallest specimen gets bullied to death by all the others—followed by the next smallest specimen and the next after that until only one remains.

The yellowtail blue damsel is usually a peaceful fish, but it may become aggressive to passive fish added to the tank after it was added.

This species reaches a maximum length of about 3 inches (8 cm) and is generally nano-tank friendly. Completely inoffensive to sessile invertebrates, it also makes an ideal reef tank inhabitant. A single specimen or a male/female pair would be suitable for a smaller tank in the range of 20 gallons. A larger tank, in the approximate range of 29 to 40 gallons, would be more appropriate for a group.

Also in keeping with its common name, *C. cyanea* is sapphire blue in overall color, but there are distinct color differences between the sexes. Females and juveniles are solid blue with clear fins, a dark line extending from the snout through the eyes, and a small dark spot at the base of the dorsal fin just

Humbug damsels will get along when they are juveniles, but the adults will fight with each other and pick on more passive fish.

ahead of the caudal peduncle. Males are also blue overall but are differentiated from females and juveniles by the presence of yellowish-orange coloration on the tail and around the mouth and chest. Mature males may also lack the dark spot at the base of the caudal fin.

Blue Body, Yellow Tail, Delightful Disposition

Another enduring aquarium favorite, the yellowtail blue damselfish, *Chrysiptera parasema*, is very similar in appearance to a male *C. cyanea*, except that on *C. parasema* the yellow coloration is usually limited to the tail (sometimes extending forward into the anal fin and the rear of the dorsal fin).

Also, *C. parasema* rarely demonstrates *C. cyanea*'s penchant for deviltry, being one of the most peaceful damsels on the market. This species is far more likely to be bullied by more assertive tankmates than to be the one doing the bullying. Order of introduction makes a difference in this regard, though. From my experience, *C. parasema* may behave aggressively toward passive species that are introduced into the tank after it but will usually ignore—or just mildly spar with—more passive species that were introduced first. Of course, you may come across individual specimens that deviate from this pattern, exhibiting more aggression than is typical, so even this somewhat

Like clownfish, juvenile domino damsels often live among the tentacles of a host anemone.

predictably peaceful species bears watching.

This nano-friendly species makes an excellent candidate for reef systems, reaching only 2½ to 3 inches (6 to 8 cm) in total length. This species can also be kept in small groups in larger tanks, provided specimens of very similar size are chosen. As with *C. cyanea*, a minimum tank size of 20 gallons is appropriate for the yellowtail blue damsel when kept singly or in mated pairs, but a larger system of at least 29 to 40 gallons would be necessary for a small group.

Bah Humbug

With its distinct black-and-white striping and iron constitution, *Dascyllus aruanus,* one of the damselfishes with "humbug" in its common name, is a long-time hobby favorite and popular choice for beginners. In nature, large aggregations of this eye-catching species will shelter among the branches of *Acropora* corals—a captivating image that just begs to be replicated in the aquarium. But, alas, keeping this species in groups in captivity ultimately leads to heartache. While juveniles will coexist peacefully in groups—and, indeed, dealers often display them this way because it shows them off to their best advantage to prospective buyers—all bets are off once they start to mature.

That is, you can expect adult specimens of *D. aruanus* to turn on any conspecifics (with a possible exception being made for mated pairs) or passive tankmates.

One must walk something of a tightrope when choosing tankmates for *D. aruanus*, or for any other belligerent damselfish species, for that matter. They must be sufficiently large and assertive to avoid being bullied but not so large and assertive that they will make a meal of the damsel.

D. aruanus reaches right around 3 inches (8 cm) in maximum length, is reef-safe, and should be afforded a tank of at least 20 gallons for an individual specimen or mated pair. Obviously, keeping this species in a community tank featuring semi-aggressive species would necessitate a much larger system if squabbling is to be kept to a minimum.

Tankmates for Cantankerous Damsels

At numerous points throughout this book, it is stated that big, feisty damsels should be housed with tankmates that are large enough and feisty enough to hold their own in the likely event that they become the target of the damsel's aggression. But in some ways, that's easier said than done. It takes a bit of a balancing act to choose tankmates that are sufficiently large and assertive to stand up to the naked aggression of a devilish damsel yet not so large and assertive that they would be inclined to view damsels as tasty snacks.

Here is a sampling of fishes that, in general, can dish it out as well as they take it when it comes to rough-and-tumble damsel tankmates:
• Larger angelfishes, such as certain *Holacanthus* and *Pomacanthus* species
• Surgeonfishes (tangs)
• Pufferfishes
• Larger dottybacks
• Hogfishes
• Larger hawkfishes
• Squirrelfishes

Keep in mind, however, that not all of the fishes on this list will be compatible with all aggressive damselfish species. All potential combinations must be evaluated for compatibility on a case-by-case basis, and it's always important to introduce specimens in ascending order of aggressiveness—with the most aggressive specimen being introduced to the aquarium last.

Juvenile jewel damsels are breathtakingly beautiful, but they grow up to be large, drab, and very aggressive fish.

I should point out that it's easy to confuse *D. aruanus* with a very similar-looking species—*Dascyllus melanurus*. Both species exhibit black-and-white zebra striping, and both are commonly called "humbug damsels." There are two obvious differences between the species, however. *D. aruanus* has a solid white tail, and its dorsal fin is almost completely black. *D. melanurus* has a black band on its tail, and the black along its dorsal fin is interrupted in the middle by white. No matter if you end up with one instead of the other, though, because the behavior and care requirements of both species are virtually identical.

Oh, Domino

Dascyllus trimaculatus, the domino or threespot damselfish, is another ubiquitous damsel that starts out as a charming, gregarious juvenile but matures into a somewhat less comely and decidedly less sociable adult. It's also hardy to the point of being practically bulletproof and is one of several unfortunate species that are often relegated to the role of piscine guinea pig for the purpose of cycling new aquariums.

Juveniles of the species are jet black with three white spots, one on the forehead and one high up on either side of the fish's body. In adults, the head spot fades away and the side spots become greatly reduced. Adult coloration is also quite variable, ranging from black to various shades of muddy gray, depending on the geographic origin and behavior of the specimen.

Juvenile *D. trimaculatus* exhibit a behavioral trait that we typically associate only with the clownfishes—that is, they are known to form commensal relationships with sea anemones. They're also known to shelter among the branches of corals and the spines of sea urchins.

D. trimaculatus achieves a respectable adult length of 5.5 inches (20 cm) and is not a good candidate for smaller aquariums. A minimum tank size of 55 to 75 gallons (210 to 280 liters) is more appropriate for this species. Also, while juveniles will cohabit peacefully in the aquarium, keeping adults in conspecific groups is out of the question, with the possible exception of a mated pair in a very large system. In addition, considerable care must be taken when choosing other tankmates for *D. trimaculatus*. House them only with large, equally assertive species, but don't be surprised to see *D. trimaculatus* take on fishes much larger than itself—wild specimens regularly attack scuba divers! In spite of its belligerence toward other fishes, this species won't harm sessile invertebrates and therefore is a potential candidate for reef systems.

A Fading Jewel

Many damselfishes have the discouraging trait of starting out as cute, colorful, well-behaved juveniles and then transforming into big, somber-hued, ill-tempered adults. A good example of these fading beauties is the jewel damselfish, *Microspathodon chrysurus*.

Exhibiting dazzling blue polka dots set against a deep blue background, the colors of this species put one in mind of gazing up at a star-filled night sky. Irresistible, right? Well, the only trouble is, those eye-catching colors are present only on juveniles of the

The bowtie damsel is another species that starts out small and beautiful only to turn dull colored and belligerent.

species. The cute 2-inch (1-cm) specimens that are commonly sold on the aquarium market are destined to reach about 8 inches (20 cm) in total length and take on a more drab yellowish-brown hue as they age. They also tend to exhibit much more territorial aggression as they reach adulthood. And if a small territorial damsel can cause chaos in a peaceful community tank, just imagine what havoc an angry 8-inch (20-cm) damsel can wreak! It's very important to consider this species's ultimate size and disposition when choosing housing and tankmates for it. An adult *M.chrysurus* will fit in well in a large system—a minimum of 75 gallons (280 liters)—housing other large, aggressive species. It's definitely not a fish for the nano tank! Nor would it be appropriate to try to keep it with others of its own kind. *M. chrysurus* is considered a reef friendly species, but considering that an 8-inch20-cm fish produces a substantial amount of dissolved pollutants through its waste, I would be wary of adding this species to most reef systems.

Tankmates for Daintier Damsels

Small, peaceful damsels, such as the various *Chromis* species and certain *Chrysiptera* and *Neopomacentrus* species, should be housed with relatively passive tankmates that aren't likely to single them out as targets for aggression. A few good choices include:

• Grammas
• Basslets
• Gobies
• Blennies
• Cardinalfishes
• Jawfishes
• Smaller hawkfishes

Compatibility issues can still arise between relatively peaceful damsels and the fishes listed here, especially if proper order of introduction—from least aggressive to most aggressive—is not observed.

True Changelings

"What on earth happened to my bowtie damselfish? When I bought it, it was one of the prettiest fish I'd ever seen! It had a light gray body with light blue fins and a bright yellow band running along its back. Then, practically overnight, it turned solid black. Is it sick or something?"

Marine aquarium dealers frequently hear questions like this from customers who have purchased *Neoglyphidodon* spp. damsels without first doing their homework on them. That's because all of the species in this genus, such as the bowtie damselfish, *N. melas,* have the same heartbreaking (for hobbyists, anyway) habit of changing from small, visually stunning juveniles to more dull-colored or monochromatic adults.

There is a subtle beauty in the adults of certain *Neoglyphidodon* species. The adult Behn's damsel, *Neoglyphidodon nigroris*, for example, is two-toned—grayish brown on the anterior half of its body and bright yellow on the posterior half. I

You can keep lemon damsels in groups if you have a large tank with plenty of hiding places.

wouldn't call its adult coloration ugly, but it can't really hold a candle to the horizontal black and gold striping of the juvenile.

On the other hand, these species' belligerence is not in question. As with *M. chrysurus*, the change to adulthood for the *Neoglyphidodon* damsels is universally accompanied by a significant increase in territorial aggression, which means that these species, ultimately, cannot be trusted to behave themselves around conspecifics or in a community of more passive species.

As these species reach 5 to 6 inches (13 to 15 cm) at maturity, a suitable minimum tank size is in the range of 55 to 75 gallons (210 to 280 liters). Reef tank suitability varies by species. For example, *N. melas* has the tendency to nibble on certain soft corals and so is not the best choice for a reef system, depending on the invertebrate species kept.

One Sweet Lemon

The aptly named lemon damsel, *Pomacentrus moluccensis*, is a cheerful uniform lemon yellow in color and reaches a maximum length of 2 to 3 inches (5 to 8 cm), making it a reasonably good choice for a nano system. A minimum tank size in the range of 20 to 29 gallons (75 to 110 liters) is recommended for this species. It's also harmless to corals and other sessile invertebrates, making it an excellent candidate for reef systems. While not overly combative as pomacentrids go (this species claims something of a middle ground when it comes to belligerence), *P. moluccensis* can be aggressive toward peaceful

Damsels That Dare To Be Different

It may seem peculiar that the juveniles of certain damselfish species, such as the various *Neoglyphidodon* species, are so remarkably different in coloration from the adults. In fact, to the casual observer, the juveniles and adults of any given species within this genus are so markedly different in color and patterning that they would appear to be representatives of two completely different species. But this strategy of changing color during the transition to adulthood, which is not uncommon among reef fishes, makes perfect sense when you think about it.

Why? Food and real estate are at a premium on the coral reefs, so reef-associated fishes will often defend these resources vigorously against any potential competitors. Since members of the same species are usually the most direct competitors for resources, territorial aggression is often directed at fishes of the same, closely related, or similar-looking species. So, if the adults of a given fish species are especially belligerent and prone to territorial aggression—as happens to be the case with the *Neoglyphidodon* species—it can be beneficial for the juveniles of the species to look very different from the adults.

tankmates, especially when confined to relatively small quarters, and is best kept one to a tank. If you want to try keeping a group of conspecifics in the same aquarium, the tank should be fairly large and provide aquascaping with an abundance of nooks and crannies that allow the individual specimens to escape one another's attention when necessary.

A Shimmering Sapphire

With its uniform metallic blue-green coloration and deeply bifurcated tail, the sapphire damsel, *Pomacentrus pavo*, somewhat favors *Chromis viridis* in general appearance (one notable difference for the sapphire damsel is the presence of a dark spot just behind the head). However, *P. pavo* is, perhaps not surprisingly, more closely akin to its congener *P. moluccensis* when it comes to sociability toward its own kind—that is, it's possible to keep it in groups or pairs, but only in large systems with plenty of hiding places. Otherwise, keep this species one to a tank and avoid overly peaceful tankmates.

Topping out at just over 4 inches (10 cm) in total length, this species requires a minimum tank size of 29 to 40 gallons (110 to 160 liters). Like *P. moluccensis*, *P. pavo* is an excellent choice for reef systems.

Out-of-the-Ordinary Damsels

In addition to the common damselfishes described above, some not-so-common species find their way into the aquarium trade from time to time. Here is a small sampling of rare and unusual damsels that you might be fortunate enough to happen upon if you keep your eyes open and that, in spite of their out-of-the-ordinary status, would make good aquarium inhabitants:

A Tiny-But-Attractive Chromis

Reaching only about 2 inches (5 cm) in total length, the midget chromis, *Chromis acares*, comes by its common name honestly. Like most other *Chromis* species, *C. acares* is peaceful toward conspecifics and tankmates and is best kept in groups of six or more. Owing to its diminutive size, a small group of this reef-safe species could easily be kept in a tank in the range of 29 gallons (110 liters). *C. acares* is a retiring species that should be kept with equally passive tankmates.

Though not among the most colorful of the *Chromis* species, *C. acares* has a delicate, understated beauty. Its pearlescent overall color is accented with a yellow patch that extends from the face to the pectoral fin, a tiny yellow dot at the base of the dorsal fin just in front of the caudal peduncle, and yellow streaks along the dorsal and ventral edges of the tail fin.

A Mouthwatering *Chromis*

The use of a common name to describe a species of fish can lead to a lot of confusion, but in the case of *Chromis dimidiata*, the chocolate-dip or two-tone chromis, a common name can really get your mouth watering! With the anterior half of its body being dark brown and the posterior half a creamy white, this species does, indeed, look as though it has been dipped in chocolate. I'll leave it to the reader's imagination (and personal cravings) to decide whether the fish is dark chocolate overall and dipped in white chocolate or vice versa.

A close relative of the lemon damsel, the sapphire damsel is similar in behavior and is also an excellent choice for a reef tank.

C. dimidiata reaches about 3.5 inches (9 cm) in total length and, if kept singly, requires an aquarium in the range of 29 gallons (110 liters). Like others in its genus, *C. dimidiata* can safely be kept in groups of six or more presuming all of the specimens are similar in size and the tank is large enough to accommodate them all and provides ample retreats.

Though *C. dimidiata* is rare in the aquarium trade, at least two very similar-looking species are commonly sold: the half-and-half chromis, *C. iomelas,* and the bicolor chromis, *C. margaritifer.* All of these two-toned *Chromis* species are good candidates for the reef aquarium.

A Delightful Deepwater Damsel

Fishes found in deeper water are inherently more difficult for collectors to capture. Hence they tend to be much more uncommon than shallow-water species in the aquarium trade. Such is the case with the blueline demoiselle, *Chrysiptera caeruleolineata*. This attractive reef-safe species, which reaches only around 2.5 inches

Lone–Wolf Damsels

With some species of damselfish, careful selection of tankmates and proper order of introduction will do little if anything to prevent endless squabbles from arising in the aquarium. Such species are found in various pomacentrid genera, such as *Stegastes, Microspathodon, Neoglyphidodon,* and *Dischistodus*. Due to their hyper-aggressive tendencies, these lone-wolf damsels are generally not considered ideal candidates for the home aquarium—unless they are given a tank all to themselves or are kept in a very large system with equally belligerent tankmates (that is, if you can find equally belligerent tankmates). Adding insult to injury, many of these lone-wolf damsels start off as small, attractive juveniles but morph into hefty, lackluster adults.

Prime examples of lone-wolf damsels that are best left out of community aquariums include:
• The Beaubrummel gregory, *Stegastes flavilatus*
• The (aptly named) giant damselfish, *Microspathodon dorsalis*
• The black damselfish, *Neoglyphidodon melas*
• The white damselfish, *Dischistodus perspicillatus*

The chocolate-dip chromis (left) and the similar and more common bicolor chromis (right) can both be kept in groups of six or more in a large tank.

(6 cm) in total length, is yellow overall and has a broad dark-blue stripe overlain with a thinner light blue stripe running along each side of its dorsal fin. A faint blush of lavender is also visible along the flanks.

C. caeruleolineata is not especially aggressive, but it may pick on more tranquil tankmates. A minimum tank size of 20 to 29 gallons (75 to 110 liters) would be appropriate for this species.

An Anthias Mimic

I chose to include *Lepidozygus tapeinosoma*, the fusilier damselfish, in my list of rare-and-unusual damsels not only because it's relatively uncommon in the aquarium trade but also because it's quite interesting as damsels go from the standpoint of behavior and morphology.

What sets this species apart behaviorally is that, in addition to forming large schools of its own kind, it's known to blend in and feed with similar-looking *Anthias* species (*Pseudanthias* spp.). This mimicry is possible because *L. tapeinosoma* is, to my eye anyway, decidedly un-damsel-like in its morphology, being much more steamlined and torpedo-shaped than you'd expect from a pomacentrid. Also, its color is very difficult to pinpoint, being highly variable depending on the species of *Anthias* it mimics and other behavioral factors.

L. tapeinosoma is relatively hardy and reef safe, reaches a maximum length of around 4 inches (10 cm), and can be kept in small conspecific groups or combined with similar-looking *Anthias* species. A tank in the range of 55 to 75 gallons (210 to 285 liters) would be appropriate for a group of this species.

8

Captive Breeding of Clownfish

Whereas most marine species sold in your local fish store are still wild-caught, all of the commonly sold clownfish species—not to mention a few that are a bit more difficult to acquire—are being bred in captivity by commercial breeders. In fact, even an experienced, determined, dedicated hobbyist can successfully breed and raise clownfishes if he or she chooses to put forth the effort.

Clownfish are of indeterminate gender until another one settles into the same anemone. Then the larger and more dominant individual becomes female and the other male.

Relatively Easy—But No Small Challenge

You'll notice that I used the adjectives "experienced," "determined," and "dedicated" to describe the hobbyist who can succeed in breeding clownfishes. That's because breeding clownfishes, while relatively easy compared to breeding other marine species, is still fraught with challenges. Don't expect the effort to be anything remotely similar to, say, breeding freshwater livebearers.

A step-by-step clownfish breeding guide is beyond the scope of this book, so what follows is a brief introduction to the various related concepts, which should give you a better understanding of the rather intense effort required to breed clownfishes and rear their young. If this chapter piques your interest and you decide you'd like to get serious about breeding clownfishes at home, I would urge you to pick up, read, and reread a copy of Joyce Wilkerson's excellent book *Clownfishes: A Guide to Their Captive Care, Breeding & Natural History* (TFH Publications, 2001), which is a veritable treasure trove of information and helpful hints for aspiring clownfish breeders.

Gender-Bending Clownfishes

Successful breeding of clownfishes requires an understanding of clownfish "gender politics." While the male of the species may have the upper hand in many animal populations, it's the female that rules the roost in any group of clownfishes. But it takes a little gender-bending to achieve this dominance.

You see, all clownfishes are born with the potential to become either male or female.

If, after settling out of the planktonic rafts and metamorphosing out of the larval stage, a juvenile clownfish settles into a host anemone and is the sole occupant, it will remain of indeterminate sex. But if you add another clownfish to the mix—i.e., another specimen settles in the anemone—the more assertive of the two will transform into a dominant female, the less assertive specimen will become the dominant male, and the two will then become a monogamous mated pair. Any newcomers that arrive in the anemone after the pair, assuming they aren't chased off, will remain non-breeding adolescents until either the dominant female or the male gets eaten or dies by other means. In that event, the male will become the dominant female and the most assertive adolescent will become the male.

This fascinating hierarchical strategy, known as protandrous hermaphroditism, ensures that reproduction will continue uninterrupted as long as two clownfish are present in the same anemone. Interestingly, while such sex changing is not unusual among marine fishes, it usually works the opposite way—with the most dominant member of the group becoming male: protogynous hermaphroditism.

Elaborating on this concept, Jay Hemdal, curator of the Toledo Zoo Aquarium, observes that it may not be valid to say a clownfish is either male or female. Rather, it should be described as an "acting male" or "acting female." He further explains that clownfishes retain both male and female sexual organs but one becomes dominant over the other under certain conditions—such as when a dominant female is removed from a colony, which

A Kiss on the Cheek

Male maroon clownfish, *Premnas biaculeatus*, have a unique way of demonstrating that they accept the dominant status of the female with whom they share an anemone or an aquarium. In addition to trembling his body to signal submissiveness, the male may also mouth her cheek spines—a behavior that looks as if he's giving her a loving peck on the cheek. Given the often over-the-top aggressiveness of a dominant female maroon clownfish, it's probably a good thing that the much smaller male has more than one way to say, "I submit!" Of course, since *P. biaculeatus* is the only clownfish equipped with cheek spines, it's the only species that exhibits this behavior—yet another characteristic that sets *P. biaculeatus* apart from the *Amphiprion* clownfishes.

would result in the next dominant fish's (usually the previously acting male) becoming the acting female.

And we think gender politics is complicated in the world of people!

Procuring a Breeding Pair

Of course, the most important component when attempting to breed any fish is a breeding male/female pair. So how do you go about acquiring a pair? This can be achieved in several ways. One is to actually purchase a known mated pair—that is, a wild pair collected from the same anemone or two tank-raised specimens that have already bonded and developed their sexes. Your dealer should be able to order a mated pair for you, or you can get a pair from various online sources if you prefer. The advantage to buying a known mated pair is that you can be fairly certain the two have already sorted out their dominance issues and, therefore, can get right to the business of procreation in your breeding tank.

Another option is to simply purchase two small juveniles, introduce them into a tank simultaneously, and allow them to mature together. After a period of vying for dominance, which can last for several weeks to months, one should become the obvious superior and the other more submissive. The more dominant specimen of the two will transform into a female and the more submissive specimen will become a male. Submission is signaled by the more passive of the pair presenting the side of its body to the dominant specimen and quivering its body—usually in response to aggressive behavior on the part of the dominant specimen.

Yet another option is to combine a larger clownfish, which would likely be a female, with a smaller specimen, which would likely be a male or an adolescent that still has the capability to transform into a male.

Wilkerson (2001) notes that putting two juvenile clownfish

To obtain a breeding pair of clownfish, you can purchase a mated pair or buy two juveniles and allow them to develop into a male–female pair.

Clownfish Gender Change: A One-Way Street

Once a clownfish specimen has made the transition from non-breeding adolescent to acting male or from acting male to acting female, there's no turning back. There are no social circumstances that will cause a female to revert to a male or a male to revert to a non-breeding adolescent.

Why does this matter to the aspiring clownfish breeder? Well, consider what would happen if you were to unwittingly put together two specimens that have already made the transformation to dominant female. There would be no way for one of the specimens to switch back to male status, and the two would never iron out their differences. So, instead of ending up with a monogamous, mated pair and their eventual offspring, you'd experience no end of squabbling.

together for the purpose of pair formation is not an option when it comes to *Premnas biaculeatus*, the maroon clownfish. With this exceedingly belligerent species, it's unlikely in this scenario that either specimen will ever yield to the other, so when attempting to breed *P. biacuelatus* your best option is to put a large and small specimen together—and, of course, provide ample refuge for the smaller specimen so it can escape the larger specimen's wrath if necessary.

Setting the Scene For Romance

Though a mated clownfish pair usually won't require much inducement to spawn, it certainly can help things along if the would-be breeder provides aquarium conditions that are conducive to clownfish canoodling. In addition to providing exceptional water quality and maintaining stable water parameters, thought must be given to the issue of tankmates as well as the physical environment afforded to the pair.

No Anemone Required

Just as clownfishes are able to survive and thrive in captivity with no host sea anemone, most will also breed successfully in captivity with no anemone present. This is a boon for would-be clownfish breeders not only because most clownfish-hosting anemones have an abysmal captive survival rate but also because attempting to keep an anemone in the spawning tank will necessitate much more exacting water conditions as well as the use of costly high-intensity lighting.

Three's a Crowd

When it comes to fish tankmates for a breeding clownfish pair, your best bet is to exclude them altogether so your breeders have the tank all to themselves. After all, you want your pair to focus their attention and energy on spawning—not on driving off interlopers or food competitors. Moreover, if they share a tank with highly active, fast-moving species, the incessant activity in the vicinity of the spawning site will keep the clownfish perpetually on edge, either discouraging them from spawning altogether or prompting them to eat their eggs after spawning.

A pair of percula clowns caring for eggs in the shelter behind their anemone. In captivity, having an anemone is not a requirement for successful spawning.

The Spawning Tank

Your spawning tank doesn't have to come with all the bells and whistles found in a display tank. A heater, protein skimmer, powerhead for water movement, and a light fixture and timer will suffice as far as equipment goes. The light timer is included not for the hobbyist's convenience but because clownfishes are less likely to spawn if regular daytime/nighttime cycles are not maintained.

A few good pieces of fully cured live rock can be used to provide biological filtration as well as a safe retreat for the clownfish pair in lieu of an anemone. The bottom of the tank can be left bare, but some breeders prefer to use at least a thin layer of substrate material in order to create a setting that is as close to natural as possible for the breeding pair.

In nature, clownfishes will typically lay their eggs on a hard, usually vertical, surface that is in close proximity to their host anemone. In aquariums, a rock, the tank glass, or any other hard substrate may be chosen for the spawning site. However, if you intend to transfer the eggs to a larval rearing tank just prior to hatching—rather than trying to capture and transfer the tiny larvae after they've hatched—it's a good idea to provide some sort of moveable substrate for the female to lay her eggs upon. Some possible choices include a piece of slate, terracotta pot, small rock, or ceramic tile. The spawning substrate should be placed close to the clownfish pair's hiding place, preferably in a vertical or near-vertical position.

Feed Them Well

To bring your clownfish into the best condition and encourage the production of healthy, viable eggs, you'll need to offer your pair a nutritious diet that includes a variety of fresh and frozen meaty items and greens. Occasional offerings of live foods, such as enriched brine shrimp or mysid shrimp, will help to kick-start spawning.

Spawning Behavior

If you observe your pair carefully, you should be able to identify certain behaviors that signal imminent spawning. For instance, you may see the male swimming up and down in front of the female or approaching her with his head up and waggling his body. If the clownfish share their tank with other fishes, the clownfish will likely kick their aggression into high gear, attacking any fish that comes too close to their potential nest site (another good reason to give your clownfish pair a tank all to themselves). As spawning draws closer, the pair will begin cleaning the chosen spawning substrate so it's ready to receive the clutch of eggs.

Once spawning commences, the female will deposit her eggs on the substrate one row at a time with the male following behind her after each row is laid to fertilize the eggs, which will number from a few hundred to well over a thousand orange-colored eggs.

They've Laid Eggs. Now What?

After the eggs have been deposited on the substrate, the male assumes the role of egg tender while the female acts as guardian. His duties include fanning the eggs with his pectoral fins to

Stable Conditions Promote Clownfish Canoodling

Changing conditions are known to trigger spawning in certain freshwater fishes. For example, *Corydoras* catfish can often be encouraged to spawn by performing a large water change using water that is several degrees cooler than the tank water. This sudden influx of cooler water simulates the onset of the rainy season, which is a good time for baby catfish to be born.

But change is generally a bad thing when you're attempting to breed clownfishes, which hail from tropical coral reefs—extremely stable environments. If you're trying to induce clownfishes to spawn, it's important to keep the temperature, specific gravity, pH, alkalinity, day/night cycles, and your feeding regimen as stable and predictable as possible.

Hatching percula clownfish eggs. Clownfish eggs take about eight days to hatch.

keep them aerated and to prevent detritus from settling on them as well as picking out any fungused or damaged eggs with his mouth. Her responsibility is simple: ruthlessly attacking anything that might upset the domestic tranquility of the nest site. Otherwise, she pretty much trusts the egg tending to the capable fins of the male.

The eggs will hatch after dark approximately eight days after they are laid, assuming the water in the breeding tank is maintained at 80°F (27°C). A lower water temperature will slow the hatching process while a higher temperature will accelerate it. If you plan to hatch the eggs in a separate tank, you'll want to move the entire substrate containing the clutch into the rearing tank about one day before hatching. You'll know hatching is imminent when the egg tips begin to take on a silvery sheen. The silver color is imparted by the developing eyes of the embryos inside the egg.

If you decide to move the substrate and eggs, you'll need to simulate the male's fanning behavior by placing a bubbling airstone below the clutch. Of course, if you don't mind putting forth the effort, there's no reason you can't allow the eggs to hatch in the breeding tank and then gently siphon or scoop out the larvae and transfer them to the rearing tank.

The Rearing Tank

Different clownfish breeders favor different larvae rearing tank configurations. For example, some recommend small rectangular tanks such as a standard 10- to 20-gallon (40- to 75- liter) tank while others favor round tanks or other round vessels. Whichever tank configuration you choose for the larvae, keep in mind that it should be small enough so that it's easy to maintain the proper density of food items in the water—in other words, so the larvae don't have to expend too much energy to find their prey—but large enough so that your larvae won't be quickly overwhelmed by their own dissolved waste.

In addition to the tank itself, you'll need an air pump and airstones to provide oxygenation, a submersible heater to maintain the desired temperature of 80°F (27°C), and a fluorescent light and timer. A substrate is neither necessary nor desirable, as it will become a repository for decomposing waste material. Nor do you need to provide live rock or other forms of aquascaping. Remember, clownfish larvae in nature aren't found residing on the reef; they drift with the tides and currents until they metamorphose into juveniles. The buildup of ammonia and other toxic dissolved

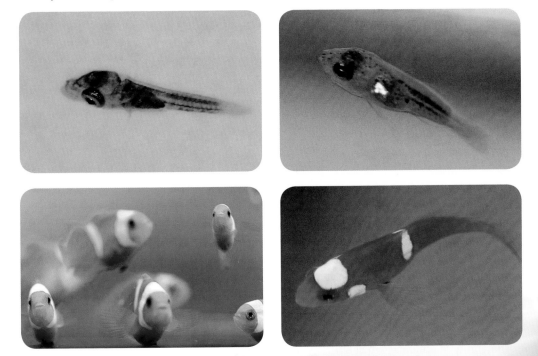

Percula clownfish larvae at various stages: (clockwise from top left) day 1, day 5, day 17, and day 31.

What About Breeding Damselfishes?

Since this book dedicates an entire chapter to the breeding of clownfishes, why doesn't it also include a chapter dedicated to damselfish breeding (the non-clownfish damsels, that is)? Wouldn't the marine aquarium hobby—not to mention wild populations of damselfishes—have much to gain from the captive breeding of damselfishes?

Indeed, captive breeding would yield healthier, hardier damselfish specimens and relieve some of the collection pressure on wild stocks. And, there's no question that dedicated experts and hobbyists out there are working diligently to put together all the pieces of the damselfish-breeding puzzle. In fact, captive damselfish spawnings are reported fairly frequently. However, with many damselfish species, one big challenge seems to stand in the way of breeding success: rearing the larvae.

Whereas clownfish larvae are relatively large when they hatch from the egg and are able to accept rotifers as their first food, the same cannot be said for most damselfishes.

As Jay Hemdal points out, most damselfish larvae require starter foods that are even smaller than the so-called "S" strain rotifers (small-strain rotifers), which means there is no readily available live food that aspiring breeders can culture. Experts have used wild plankton to feed and rear damselfish larvae, but this is certainly not a cost-effective option when you're attempting to breed fishes that typically fetch a rather modest price on the market.

The good news is, more and more breakthroughs are being made in the captive breeding of damselfishes. For example, Tony Gardner (2008) has reported the successful rearing of the golden damselfish, *Amblyglyphidodon aureus*, at Atlantis Marine World, "with a success rate approaching 100 percent, using rotifers as a first food."

As further advances are made in the captive breeding of damselfishes and, hopefully, commercially viable aquaculture programs come into being, it is hoped that hobbyists will lend their financial support to these programs by purchasing captive-raised specimens over wild-caught whenever they have the option—even if they should cost a few dollars more.

pollutants in the rearing tank should be prevented by performing large daily water changes.

Wilkinson (2001) also recommends darkening the sides of the rearing tank with some sort of non-reflective cover, such as black construction paper or black plastic, for at least the first five or six days, as light leaking in from the sides could interfere with the ability of the larvae to catch prey. She notes that "Clownfish have not evolved with light streaming at them from all sides, as it does in an aquarium. Larvae have sideways-facing eyes and seem unable to sight prey when surrounded by side lighting."

Because clownfish larvae are drawn to both light and warm water, a submerged aquarium heater that contains a pilot light poses a double threat to them. To prevent the larvae from congregating around the heater and, hence, getting cooked, either conceal the pilot light with electrical tape or choose a model that is encased in a plastic sheath. Also, place an airstone beneath the heater so the rising bubbles create a current that disperses the heat.

Feeding the Larvae

Once the larvae have hatched and are settled in their rearing tank, the real work begins—feeding all those tiny hungry mouths. But I should emphasize that by first discussing the hatching of clownfish eggs and appropriate housing for the larvae, I've put the proverbial cart before the horse. That's because by the time you have larvae on your hands, you should already be prepared to provide a steady supply of live food for them.

First Food For the Larvae

Live marine rotifers, specifically the species *Branchionus plicatilis*, are the ideal first food for those miniscule clownfish larvae. Rotifers are microscopic—or just barely visible—planktonic organisms that can be purchased, either as live cultures or dormant cysts. Most are found in fresh water, but *B. plicatilis* is a euryhaline species, which means it can tolerate a wide range of salinities. While not a natural food source for clownfish larvae, rotifers are the perfect size to fit their mouths (for reference, they're approximately ½ the size of newly hatched brine shrimp), they're easy for the clownfish larvae to catch, and they're a pretty decent source of nutrition.

However, in order to provide enough rotifers to sustain clownfish larvae, it's necessary for the breeder to maintain an ongoing culture of them in a small aquarium or other container dedicated to that purpose. That's not such a simple task, as you have to strike a balance between the size of the rotifer culture you're maintaining and the feeding demand of the clownfish larvae. If the rotifer population increases beyond the demand of the larvae, the water quality in the culture tank can plummet, causing the whole culture to crash. Conversely, if the culture doesn't generate sufficient quantities of rotifers, the clownfish larvae will starve.

The rotifers must be introduced to the larvae rearing tank in sufficient numbers so each larva can spot and hunt down, according to Wilkinson (2001), somewhere between

500 and 1,000 of them each day without having to exhaust itself in the effort. It stands to reason, then, that the larger the larvae rearing tank, the more rotifers you'll need to introduce in order to reach and maintain the appropriate density.

Food to Feed the Food

Once again, however, I've put the cart before the horse. You won't have any marine rotifers to feed your larvae unless you've got on hand a regular supply of food for the rotifers. That's right; you have to provide a food to feed the food that will be fed to your larvae. So what food would be small enough to feed microscopic rotifers, and how do you go about acquiring it? The answer is microalgae, and, as with marine rotifers, you'll have to maintain an ongoing culture of it in your home if you plan to breed any of the clownfishes.

Culturing microalgae, or green water, essentially involves adding a small portion of a microalgae starter culture (available in disk or liquid form through aquaculture supply houses) to a medium consisting of salt water and microalgae fertilizer. The mixture is then placed under lights and aerated with a bubbling airstone. As the culture matures, the color of the water will change from light green to dark green, which indicates that the green water is ready to be fed to the rotifer tank.

Breeders typically culture several batches of green water at once, for example, in a series of plastic 2-liter soda bottles, so that there's always a ready supply of microalgae. When one culture is fed to the rotifers, part of it is held back and used to get another culture under way.

The Second Course

So, now you've got two sets of cultures going—rotifers to feed the larvae and green water to feed the rotifers. That ought to be enough effort on your part to keep any fish larvae alive and thriving, right? Well, it'll get them by for the first five days of life, anyway. After that, the larvae will need to move on to bigger fare, a prey item most freshwater fish breeders are well acquainted with—namely brine shrimp nauplii.

Brine shrimp eggs are readily available, and you can culture them in commercially manufactured hatcheries or construct your own hatchery using a plastic soda bottle and an airstone. The larvae should be fed brine shrimp nauplii until they metamorphose into juveniles. At that point, it's time to start weaning them onto other appropriately sized offerings, such as finely crushed flake and freeze-dried foods. Of course, as the juveniles increase in size, you can begin to offer larger and more varied food items.

Some species of clowns are rarely tank raised, such as the white-bonnet clown, *A. leucokranos*. This wild pair is tending its eggs.

Is Clownfish Breeding For You?

If this rather rudimentary description of the clownfish-breeding process hasn't frightened you off and the idea of having to culture three different types of food—green water, rotifers, and brine shrimp—to sustain the larvae strikes you as an interesting challenge, clownfish breeding might be right up your alley. If so, I would urge you to do plenty of additional reading and research to familiarize yourself with the various tools and techniques breeders use as well as the obstacles and frustrations you're likely to encounter at the various stages of the process. There's no question, however, that those who do rise to the challenge of clownfish breeding not only experience an unparalleled sense of accomplishment but also make a significant contribution to the well-being of wild clownfish populations by helping to reduce collection pressure.

9

The Beginning of a Rewarding Experience

A well-cared-for clownfish or damselfish can bring its keeper many years of enjoyment. In fact, pomacentrids have been known to live well beyond a decade in captivity, sometimes living as long as—or even longer than—the family dog or cat. As I mentioned in an earlier chapter, the little finger-nipping percula clownfish that resides in my 75-gallon (285-liter) reef tank has been alive and kicking for almost 12 years as of this writing. Not to mention that it shares its quarters with a little yellowtail blue damsel that was purchased on the same day! Not a bad lifespan for a couple of 2-inch (5-cm) fishes, and they're not showing any signs of slowing down yet!

Pomacentrids have the potential to live for a decade or more. Yours will only thrive for that long if you are a conscientious aquarist.

But if a pomacentrid's potential longevity is to be realized, it's incumbent upon you, the marine aquarium hobbyist, to provide the best possible conditions for the clownfish or damselfish in your care. To achieve this, you should:

- Know exactly what you're getting yourself into. Research the care requirements and relative aggressiveness of any pomacentrid specimen before buying it.
- Avoid unwittingly introducing pathogens or parasites into your display tank and help ease your new pomacentrid's transition to aquarium life by following proper quarantine and acclimation protocols.
- House your specimen in an appropriately sized aquarium. Remember, even peaceful schooling pomacentrids will bicker with one another when kept in overly cramped quarters.
- Choose compatible tankmates, avoiding any species that is likely to view pomacentrids as lunch as well as any species that will be inclined to harass or be harassed by your clownfish or damsel.
- Introduce specimens according to their level of aggression—with more peaceful species being added ahead of more aggressive ones. Given the pomacentrids' well-earned reputation for aggressiveness, with some noteworthy exceptions, of course, it's often the damsel or clownfish that should be introduced last.

- When keeping pomacentrids in groups (assuming it's a species that can be kept in groups), choose specimens that are as close to the same size as possible and put all of them into your aquarium simultaneously.
- Offer a nutritious, varied menu suitable for an omnivore, such as small or finely chopped meaty foods of marine origin (frozen and fresh), algae-based flakes and/or pellets, staple flakes and/or pellets, and frozen omnivore and herbivore formulas. Avoid the all-too-common habit of feeding only one type of food out of convenience.
- Maintain stable, appropriate water parameters—temperature, specific gravity, pH, etc. Pomacentrids may be able to tolerate fluctuations in water chemistry and quality that would prove deadly to more sensitive fishes, but they'll live much longer, healthier lives if afforded optimal living conditions.
- Perform regular partial water changes to keep dissolved pollutants to a minimum and to help maintain the stable parameters discussed in the previous point.
- Of course, knowing what to look for in a healthy specimen, knowing how to spot the symptoms of diseases that are common to pomacentrids, and making the commitment to purchase captive-bred over wild-caught specimens whenever possible will also help ensure that you end up with a long-lived clownfish or damselfish.

    If you're new to the marine aquarium hobby—or you're a seasoned hobbyist who hasn't yet had the opportunity to keep a clownfish or damselfish—hopefully this book has provided all the essential information you'll need in order to successfully maintain pomacentrids in captivity. On the other hand, if you're an old salt who hasn't experienced the joy of keeping pomacentrids in a long while, I hope the information contained here has reawakened your interest in this fascinating family of fishes. In either case, you can rest assured that the purchase of a healthy clownfish or damselfish is just the start of a long, rewarding experience!

References

Fenner, R. M., "*Entacmaea quadricolor;* Bubble Tip (BTA), Rose Anemones in Captive Systems," *Diversity of Aquatic Life Series,* WetWebMedia.com.

Fenner, R. M. *The Conscientious Marine Aquarist,* TFH Publications (Microcosm/TFH Professional Series), 2001.

Gardner, T., "Breeder's Net: Rearing the Golden Damselfish, *Amblyglyphidodon aureus,* A Promising Candidate for Aquaculture," *Advanced Aquarist's Online Magazine,* April 2008.

Goemans, B.; L. Ichinotsubo; M. A. Moe, *The Marine Fish Health and Feeding Handbook: The Essential Guide to Keeping Saltwater Species Alive and Thriving,* TFH Publications (Microcosm/TFH Professional Series), 2008.

Hemdal, J. F., *Aquarium Fish Breeding,* Barron's Educational Series, 2003.

Hemdal, J. F., personal communication.

Michael, S. W., *Damselfishes & Anemonefishes: The Complete Illustrated Guide to Their Identification, Behaviors, and Captive Care,* TFH Publications (Microcosm/TFH Professional Series), 2008.

Wilkerson, J. D., *Clownfishes: A Guide to Their Captive Care, Breeding & Natural History,* TFH Publications (Microcosm/TFH Professional Series), 2001.

Resources

Magazine & Online Forum

Tropical Fish Hobbyist
1 TFH Plaza
3rd & Union Avenues
Neptune City, NJ 07753
E-mail: info@tfh.com
www.tfhmagazine.com

Internet Resources

Aquaria Central
www.aquariacentral.com

Aquarium Hobbyist
www.aquariumhobbyist.com

Microcosm Aquarium Explorer
www.microcosmaquariumexplorer.com

Wet Web Media
www.wetwebmedia.com

Associations and Societies

Federation of American Aquarium
Societies (FAAS)
E-mail: Jbenes01@yahoo.com
www.faas.info

Marine Aquarium Societies of North
America (MASNA)
http://www.masna.org/

Books

Fenner, Robert. *The Conscientious Marine Aquarist*. Microcosm/T.F.H. Publications, Inc.

Kurtz, Jeff. *Saltwater Aquarium Problem Solver*. T.F.H. Publications, Inc.

Kurtz, Jeff with David E. Boruchowitz. *The Simple Guide to Marine Aquariums, Second Edition*. T.F.H. Publications, Inc.

Hellweg, Michael R. *Culturing Live Foods*. T.F.H. Publications, Inc.

Paletta, Michael. *The New Marine Aquarium: Step-By-Step Setup & Stocking Guide*. Microcosm/T.F.H. Publications, Inc.

Ward, Ashley. *Questions & Answers on Saltwater Aquarium Fishes*. T.F.H. Publications, Inc.

Index

About the Author

Jeff Kurtz is a freelance writer and editor who lives in Toledo, Ohio with his wife, Melissa, and two children, Aidan and Hannah. In addition to editing the

health-and-fitness publication *Healthy Living News*, he is a contributing editor for *Tropical Fish Hobbyist* magazine and has authored or coauthored several additional books for TFH Publications, including *The Simple Guide to Marine Aquariums*, *The Simple Guide to Mini-Reef Aquariums*, *The Super Simple Guide to Landscaping Your Garden Pond*, and the *Saltwater Aquarium Problem Solver*. An avid aquarium hobbyist for almost three decades, Jeff focuses primarily on marine fish and invertebrates but enjoys freshwater fishkeeping, as well.